RECIPE FOR HAPPINESS

9 essential ingredients for a happy life

Frederika Roberts

Printed in the U.K. by Charlesworth Press, Flanshaw Way, Flanshaw Lane, Wakefield, WF2 9LP

To Chris

Be happy!

Frederika

Credits
Photographs: Frederika Roberts, Charlotte Roberts

Please see acknowledgement section for full thanks to everyone who has made this book possible.
Special thanks go to the following Authors/Researchers/Speakers (listed in alphabetical order) for their kind responses and support. The web addresses were accurate at the time of going to press.

Nigel Risner www.nigelrisner.com
Gretchen Rubin www.gretchenrubin.com
Debra Searle www.debrasearle.com

For Charlie and Hannah

"It is true that, on having reflected for some years now that scarcely anything was to be gained by being so, I have begun to be somewhat merry because I have been told that that is good for one's health."
Voltaire

"If happiness is indeed a way of being, a state of consciousness and inner freedom, there is essentially nothing to prevent us from achieving it."
Matthieu Ricard

Contents

Introduction

Why write about Happiness?

> *"Striving to be happy is a serious, legitimate and worthy aim."*
> *Sonja Lyubomirsky*

Why do some people radiate happiness whereas others seem to carry the weight of the world on their shoulders? What is it that makes us happy and why is it so important? Is happiness something that some people are naturally endowed with, or is it a skill that can be learnt?

All my life, people have commented on my 'happy disposition' and I have often been asked how I maintain this cheery attitude when life has thrown some pretty traumatic events at me, so I decided to investigate the subject of happiness further and share my findings so that others could apply them to their own lives.

Having looked in more detail at the ingredients of my personal Recipe for Happiness, I began to see patterns emerging and realised that there were some fundamental elements - some essential ingredients - that make up overall happiness. I realised that there was more to happiness than meets the eye. Thus began a journey of discovery. I read books and research papers and explored themes around the topic, such as:

What is the difference between joy and happiness?
How do optimism and pessimism influence a person's happiness?
Where does gratitude fit in?
Is pleasure the same thing as happiness?
Is happiness a short-term or long-term experience?
Does happiness come from within or is it created externally?

Psychology used to focus on what is wrong with people's psyches. The main focus was on treating ailments of the mind, on reversing depression and returning to normality. The late 1990s, however, saw the advent of 'positive psychology', pioneered by Martin Seligman. This signalled a new approach and focus in the study of human psychology; a focus on the enjoyment of life, on fulfilment, on happiness. This has led to a recognition that happiness leads to success and luck, rather than the other way around.

"We now know that happiness is the precursor to success, not merely the result. And that happiness and optimism actually fuel performance and achievement – giving us the competitive edge that I call the Happiness Advantage."
Shaun Achor

Happiness is crucially important to our well-being and is also a fundamental element in our ability to be successful in life. Happiness has been shown, in recent years, to be essential to success in our working lives; happy people have been shown to have better health, to live longer and have lower absenteeism. Happy people have also been shown to achieve more. Whether you run your own business or work for someone else or have employees of your own, therefore, understanding happiness is a crucial business tool. Many people, however, don't know how to be happy or happier.

This book is intended to serve as a guide, a roadmap to happiness. Whether you are a naturally happy person or happiness is something you need to work a little bit harder at, there are essential happiness ingredients that everybody can add to their lives in order to boost their happiness level, whatever their starting point.

How to read this book

Happiness above everything is a choice. In order to be happy, you need to decide to be happy, to want to be happy. I hope that by picking up this book you have already taken that first step; you have decided that you want to be happy or happier. You want strategies to boost your happiness levels when perhaps you're feeling a bit low. With that in mind, the first chapter – 'Happiness is a Deliberate State of Mind' - is the essential chapter to read as a starting point. If you don't make that conscious decision to be happy, you can't implement any of the strategies outlined within the book. You need to make that decision; you need to take that first step. Having done that, you can read the other chapters in whichever order you want to as they work very well as stand-alone 'chunks' for you to digest.

Within the pages that follow, you will find references

to specific scientific research, inspirational quotes and a selection of anecdotes – from people I have interviewed as well as from my own life - to support the principles underpinning the Recipe for Happiness. Each chapter also includes some simple exercises for you to carry out in order to help you in your pursuit of happiness. Coming back to the point that happiness is your choice – something you need to decide to take into your own hands - you need to take action. You can't wait for happiness to come to you, to simply happen to you. The simple exercises / actions contained in each chapter are designed to help you boost your happiness levels and get you on the road to improved fundamental happiness.

At the end of the book, I have included a brief list of suggested further reading. I have read – and referenced in this book – some of the books listed, while others are on my 'to read' list for the future. If you have any of your own recommendations or any other comments or suggestions, please e-mail me at **fred@happiness-speaker.co.uk**.

Each chapter also includes a recipe for you to cook and enjoy.

Why the recipes?

> *"If you really want to make a friend, go to someone's house and eat with him... the people who give you their food give you their heart."*
> *César Chávez*

Food is so much more than nutrition to Italians. Food is

about family. Food is about friendships. Food is about being sociable. Watch a group of Italians around a dinner table, taking their time over their meal, sharing laughter and animated conversation, and you will see a picture of happiness.

> *"In Italy, more than anywhere else, food is life; It's family, it's tradition, it's pleasure, it's passion, it's style and it's confidence."*
> Nigella Lawson, Nigellissima (TV Series, BBC)

As an Italian, I have always found food to be central to my life, my social activities and my family. Food is an integral component to my fundamental happiness. For me, it isn't just about eating the food. Cooking, sharing recipes, talking about food; these are all essential ingredients to my Recipe for Happiness. I already share my recipes, along with traditional Italian recipes passed down from generation to generation, with readers worldwide via my food blog and I couldn't write a book about happiness without including mentions of some of my favourite recipes. I hope you will enjoy cooking them, sharing them and eating them as much as my friends, family and I do.

If you want to experience more of my recipes, please visit my blog: **www.gloriouslygoodfood.com**

Happiness is a Deliberate State of Mind

"If you want to be happy, be."
Leo Tolstoy

Happiness can be looked at on two levels. There is the happiness, or elation, felt when something great happens in our lives; this is a temporary state of being that doesn't necessarily impact on a person's general position on the happiness continuum. Then there is fundamental happiness; an over-arching state of being that allows us to overcome the most tremendous difficulties and 'bounce back' to our natural happy state. Both types of happiness are worth striving for, not least because the former can have a tremendous impact on the latter. The ultimate goal, however, is fundamental happiness for its long-term effect on our enjoyment of life.

"By happiness I mean here a deep sense of flourishing that arises from an exceptionally healthy mind. This is not a mere pleasurable feeling, a fleeting emotion, or a mood, but an optimal state of being. Happiness is also a way of interpreting the world, since while it may be difficult to change the world, it is always possible to change the way we look at it."
Matthieu Ricard

Ashley W, *whose wife was diagnosed with terminal cancer in late 2008 and lost her fight in August 2011, describes happiness as follows:*

"Is it possible to remain in this state continuously? I don't believe so. We experience peaks and troughs as we go through life. The nearest possible we can get is a combination of sometimes total happiness and always being comfortable in our own skin- "contentment".

In her book, The How of Happiness, Sonja Lyubomirsky outlines the result of years of research she and her colleagues undertook into what determines happiness[1]. Their original article referenced previous research findings, which established that, in determining our overall happiness level, 50% is set by genetic predisposition. That still leaves 50% to be determined by other factors. Surprisingly, only 10% of our overall happiness level is determined by external circumstances (economic and political factors, health, and so on). 40% of our overall happiness level, according to Sonja and her colleagues, is therefore determined by our 'intentional activity'. This means that, even though some of us are genetically predisposed to be on a lower point on the happiness scale, we can deliberately - intentionally - move ourselves to the happiest point on the scale within our natural range.

The key to happiness lies not in changing our genetic make-up (which is impossible) and not in changing our circumstances (i.e. seeking wealth or attractiveness or better colleagues, which is usually impractical), but in our daily 'intentional activities'. Sonja Lyubomirsky

1. Lyubomirsky, S., Sheldon, K.M., and Schkade, D. (2005), 'Pursuing Happiness: The architecture of sustainable change', Review of General Psychology, 9, 111-131

Let's therefore explore what those 'intentional activities' are.

Have you ever had one of those mornings?

Your alarm goes off. It's early; too early. It's dark and cold. Before you even leave your bed, you can hear the rain pounding on your window. You get up, sleepily, and stub your toe on the end of the bed. You hobble into the bathroom, muttering choice expletives, and as you get ready to brush your teeth, your toothbrush falls into the toilet!

Do you say to yourself "It's going to be one of those days"?

Many people use negative self-talk without even thinking about it. Many take it further; the self-talk becomes conversation. They tell their partners over breakfast, they tell their colleagues when they get to work, they may even post on Facebook: "It's going to be one of those days!"

Days like these have one thing in common. The early morning proclamation that it's going to be "one of those days" becomes a self-fulfilling prophecy. Having told yourself that you will have a bad day, you end up having a bad day.

This is because our thought processes are programmable and we love to be right. The reality is that most days are a mixture of good, bad and indifferent events. If we tell our subconscious, however, that we're going to have a bad day, it gets to work to 'help' us achieve just that. It filters out the positive, so we notice only the negative; with each additional negative event brought to our attention by our ever-helpful subconscious, we receive confirmation that we were right.

"Whether you think you can or you think you can't – you're right."
Henry Ford

What would happen if you gave your sub-conscious a different message and consequently gave it a different task? Imagine the scenario again. You get up. It is too early. It is dark. It is cold and wet. Your toe is throbbing, your toothbrush is now in the bin and you have washed your hands very thoroughly after fishing it out. This is definitely not the way you wanted your day to start. Try telling yourself, out loud – because our brain takes more notice when we hear, as well as think, a message – "That's all the bad stuff over with for today. It can only get better from this point forward. Today is going to be a great day. Today, I'm going to be happy".

In his book 'The Happiness Advantage', Shaun Achor talks about the brain having a "spam file" that surplus information goes into. He explains that scientists have estimated that we only remember 1% of the many pieces of information we receive and we therefore "see what we look for and miss the rest".

Therefore, if we look for the positive, most of the negative will go into this so-called "spam file".

*"Seeking happiness outside ourselves is like
waiting for sunshine in a cave facing north."
Tibetan Saying*

There are, of course, circumstances in life that are
bigger than a stubbed toe or ruined toothbrush. You
may genuinely have a bad week, or month, or even
year.

Unfulfilling jobs, the breakdown of business or personal
relationships, debts spiralling out of control, the list
could be endless.

These are still circumstances you have the power to
change. Sometimes it's complicated, even expensive
to change these situations or remove yourself from
them, but it is possible. Change can be uncomfortable
and feel awkward. You may have to make short-term
sacrifices and changes that don't come naturally. As
human beings, we don't like the uncomfortable and
awkward, so it's often easier to maintain the status
quo. People around you may not like the changes you
are making, especially if they affect them, so they may
put barriers in your way. Ultimately, though, the power,
but also the responsibility, for your happiness is yours.
Happiness, like anything else worthwhile in life, requires
some effort on your part.

*"Happiness is the consequence of personal
effort. You fight for it, strive for it, insist upon it, and
sometimes even travel around the world looking
for it. You have to participate relentlessly in the
manifestations of your own blessings. And once
you have achieved a state of happiness, you*

must never become lax about maintaining it,
you must make a mighty effort to keep swimming
upward into that happiness forever, to stay afloat
on top of it."
Elizabeth Gilbert

Making changes in your life now can have a future
beneficial effect when you remember them and when
you reflect on the positive effect those changes have
had on your life and you relive the point in time when
you achieved your happy outcome.

"A technique I often rely on is to re-live a moment
of achievement or happiness."
Debra Searle

Ashley F *told me of her determined effort to*
change her circumstances to happier ones:
Until she met her husband, Ashley had been in an
unhappy relationship, her job was unfulfilling and
her family were pulling her in all directions, though
she didn't think of herself as terribly unhappy.
Then she met Steve and this was the trigger for
change that she needed. They met while they
were working for the same company. They had
the same interests. Ashley suddenly realised how
unhappy she'd been.

As their relationship progressed, they decided
it would be best if they didn't work together, so
Steve left his job and moved to another one.
One day, he told her that there was an opening
in Derbyshire, 160 miles north of where they lived.
They decided to go for it. Within a short space of

time, Ashley had changed her relationship, left her job and her friends behind and moved to a new part of the country. It took courage to make that change, but she was much happier as a result.

Over to you...
Take a look at circumstances in your past that you moved away from. Write down at least one example.

Ask yourself how you felt once you had successfully made the change.

Write down the answer, then take some time to re-live the feeling as vividly as you can. Bring that moment back to life; bring back the feelings you felt at the time. Enjoy that feeling of achievement once again and congratulate yourself on your success.

Remind yourself of that feeling the next time you need to make a change in your life and feel uncomfortable or scared to take the first steps.

There are life events, of course, that you have no control over. Some events are scary, life-changing and definitely not fair.

How do you pick yourself up from rock bottom?

You may have no control over the events that have turned your world upside down, but you do have a choice about how you react to these events.

"Everything can be taken from a man but one thing: the last of the human freedoms – to choose one's attitude in any given set of circumstances, to choose one's own way. […] Any man can […] decide what shall become of him – mentally and spiritually. He may retain his human dignity even in a concentration camp."
Viktor Frankl

"Choose Your Attitude has become more than just a motto to me – it is a way of life. […] I refused to let myself dwell on how bad the situation was by making myself choose an appropriate attitude every morning, because that was the one thing I did have a choice about."
Debra Searle

Realising you have choice is the first step to overcoming terrifying obstacles and circumstances. My moment of clarity, of realisation that it really does come down to choice, came when my eldest daughter was diagnosed with multiple and complicated heart defects at birth. I had a choice: How did I want to live my life? What life did I want for my daughter? How were we going to move forward as a family? We knew she would need open heart surgery at a very early age and the future was scary and uncertain, but we wanted her to have a happy life. We wanted our family to have a happy life.

For me, this was a crucial realisation. I could dwell on the unfairness of it all, paralyse myself with fear over the unknown future, or I could re-frame my concept of 'normal' and be grateful for the fact that I had a beautiful baby daughter. I chose to be happy and enjoy every great moment. I chose to worry about the scary stuff when I had to worry about it and do everything in my power to help Charlie have a good life, an enjoyable life, a happy life. When I was told, mid-pregnancy, that my second-daughter had a life-threatening heart condition, I faced an even more difficult choice. Her condition was so rare, so complex and dangerous, that we were advised to consider a termination.

Strengthened by our experiences with Charlie, and having found – with my mother's help – an exceptional surgical and medical team at Birmingham Children's Hospital, my husband and I chose to continue with the pregnancy. I also chose to enjoy every day of the rest of my pregnancy; every kick, every bit of heartburn, every little back twinge, because, whilst the outlook for my daughter after birth was uncertain at best, she was safe for the remainder of my pregnancy. When she was born, my husband and I were happy and grateful that we were lucky enough to have another amazing daughter, Hannah.

Did I just take these momentous life events in my stride? Of course not. They were painful and terrifying. I was angry – and at times still am – and frustrated. I was afraid and the fear bubbles under the surface, waiting for any opportunity to erupt. Every time we take the girls for a check-up, every time another challenge comes our way, every time I stop and think about it for too long. I realised very early on though that these emotions, whilst natural and understandable, would not serve me very well in the long term. I needed a coping strategy. I needed to be able to get on with life and my daughters deserved to have happy lives, unhindered by my fears and anger at the situation we found ourselves in. I therefore made a conscious decision to focus on the positives. I decided to be happy and grateful for what I have, not resentful for what I don't have. It worked. I am happy. I am grateful. The girls lead happy lives. Family life is good.

Hannah (left) and Charlie (right) on holiday in Italy in July 2013

Gratitude – part 1

I am fundamentally happy because I am grateful. I am grateful that I have two amazing daughters when there are people who desperately want children and can't have them. I am grateful not to have to go through any of the difficult and terrifying times on my own as I have a wonderfully supportive husband by my side. I am even grateful for the fact that, if my daughters had to have medical conditions, their conditions affect their hearts; as strange as that may sound. The heart is the focus of much medical research and we have already benefited from a number of life-saving advances in medicine and surgery for our daughters.

Life doesn't always follow a set recipe. Plans and circumstances change. Sometimes you're not given the ingredients you had hoped for. The end result can still be delicious though; the meal you end up with may even be better than you originally expected. If you make the effort to sprinkle little happiness ingredients into your daily life, you can achieve fundamental happiness; the kind of happiness that will allow you to pick yourself up from even the bleakest of circumstances or events.

Over to you...
What are the little happiness ingredients in your life?

Maybe it's a great comedy DVD that has you laughing before all the punch-lines because you've watched it so often. Perhaps it's a long-overdue 'phone call with a friend that always puts a smile on your face. Or maybe you like curling up under the covers with a great book and shutting out the cold and the rain.

Make a list of your little happiness ingredients, of all the little things that put a smile on your face. When you're having 'one of those days', refer back to your list and pick an ingredient or two , then add it into your personal recipe for happiness for that day. You will feel better as a result!

Wherever your genetic predisposition places you on the happiness scale, you still have that crucial 40% of influence over your overall happiness. You have the power to make those choices, to carry out 'intentional activities' that will move you to the top of your natural happiness range.

"Happiness, more than anything, is a state of mind, a way of perceiving and approaching ourselves and the world in which we reside."
Sonja Lyubomirsky

Spaghetti al pomodoro fresco e basilico

Spaghetti al pomodoro fresco e basilico
(Spaghetti with fresh tomatoes and basil)

This recipe is one of my little happiness ingredients. To me, it just shouts out "It's Summer!" even when it isn't, and always puts a smile on my face.

It is a feast for so many senses; sight, smell and of course taste. The colours, the scent, the flavours; everything comes together in glorious harmony to lift my mood. It is so easy and quick to prepare that it is the perfect food for an impromptu get-together with friends (another of my favourite little happiness ingredients).

Next time you wake up to a dark, cold, rainy day, make this recipe the little happiness ingredient in your day. When you are enjoying a fantastically sunny, gloriously warm and fun summer day with family or friends, add this little happiness ingredient to the mix and make your day even better.

Ingredients (quantities according to taste and appetite)

- Spaghetti
- Fresh tomatoes, chopped up
- Fresh garlic, finely chopped or crushed (about half a clove per person, but this is subject to individual taste)
- Fresh basil leaves, torn or roughly chopped
- A generous splash of extra virgin olive oil
- A few drops of vegetable/cooking oil for the

pasta cooking water
- Sea salt to taste
- Coarse sea salt for the pasta cooking water
- Optional: Ground chilli flakes, to taste (add to individual servings at the dinner table)

Method

Bring a big pan of water to the boil, add a handful of coarse sea salt and a drop of oil (no need for olive oil here, it's just to stop the pasta from sticking).

Put enough spaghetti into the boiling water for however many people you're feeding (approx. 150-200g per person if it's a one-course meal, depending on how great their appetites are) and cook to 'al dente' consistency (cooked but not soggy, with a little bit of 'bite' left).

While the pasta is cooking, chop the tomatoes and finely chop or crush the garlic.

Place these into a big bowl and add the chopped or torn basil leaves.

Season with sea salt (to taste) and add a generous helping of excellent quality extra virgin olive oil.

When the pasta is cooked, drain and immediately transfer into the bowl holding the tomatoes, basil & garlic.

Toss everything together and serve immediately!

For those that enjoy a bit of spice, provide ground chilli flakes (we have ours in a salt/pepper mill set to its finest setting) and each individual can add these to their own portion, to taste.

Enjoy!

Ask for Help

"Oh, I get by with a little help from my friends;
Mm, I get high with a little help from my friends."
John Lennon and Paul McCartney (Song 'With a
little help from my friends' by The Beatles)

Asking for help is often a difficult thing for people to
do, yet in an emergency, you would exclaim 'Help!' as
'an appeal for urgent assistance'[2]   .

There are many situations in life, however, when we
need help – whether practical, financial, emotional, or
even just the answer to something we don't know - yet
we often find it difficult to ask for it.

Paradoxically, though, helping others makes us feel
good, so by asking for help, we can help others feel
good. It may be a somewhat circular argument, but it
works.

"When you commit acts of kindness, you may
begin to view yourself as an altruistic and
compassionate person. This new identity can
promote a sense of confidence, optimism and
usefulness."
Sonja Lyubomirsky

"Selfless good deeds don't exist."
Joey Tribbiani (character in 'Friends' TV Sitcom,
NBC, Season 5 Episode 4)

2. Source: http://www.oxforddictionaries.com

I couldn't resist including a quote from 'Friends' as it's one of my ultimate feel-good TV shows; one of the little happiness ingredients I like to sprinkle onto my life on a regular basis. In the episode I've taken the above quote from, Phoebe keeps trying to prove to Joey that there are selfless good deeds. Just when she thinks she's succeeded, she finds delight in how her latest good deed has helped his career and realises with dismay that she has benefited from her 'selfless' act after all.

When helping others makes us feel so good, why do we struggle so much to give others the opportunity to help us and feel happier themselves in the process?

I asked for help on this topic – I liked the irony of this – via social media and received some interesting answers. These are the main reasons people gave me for not asking for help:

- We need to learn to ask for help as it doesn't come naturally
- The feeling we need to do everything ourselves out of a sense of pride / feeling that if we can't do it ourselves, we've failed; that we shouldn't have to ask a question as we should know the answer ourselves
- Worry about being indebted to people or having the help we've received "thrown back in our faces" in future (in fact, one respondent poignantly stated that some prefer to sink on their own rather than having to feel grateful to anyone)
- Fear (of rejection, of looking stupid)
- Shame
- Worry about imposing on / burdening others

Lisa's husband died suddenly as a result of a tragic car accident nine years ago. Eventually, she fell in love again, only to find that she and her partner couldn't conceive children naturally. After two years of IVF heartbreak, she was finally pregnant with twins, who were then born 13 weeks early. The first few months of their lives were traumatic for Lisa and her partner. Here is her response to my question:

"I think being the eldest sibling I felt I'd always been there to support and listen to my family members. After losing Peter so suddenly, my family and friends were amazing at supporting me, but it was the first time I'd ever really needed help and I found it very difficult not being the 'strong one' and feeling I should be able to cope. Having my loved ones drop everything and come and be with me during those dark days meant so much. When the twins arrived early, again we were overwhelmed by generosity and were given so much help but this time around I found it much easier to accept and even ask for help. Maybe easier because it was for my babies rather than just for 'just me'. "

If we do find it easier to ask for help on behalf of someone else, perhaps this has something to do with the point Sonja Lyubomirsky made. We're being altruistic by asking for help on behalf of others, so we don't put the same obstacles in our own way as when we ourselves need help.

Fran also raised some interesting points about our

general reluctance, as human beings, to ask for help:

In the case of financial help, Fran felt that she shouldn't need help from her parents anymore; she's an adult. She only asked her father for financial help when she was absolutely desperate.

In a professional setting, Fran felt that sometimes there is the old adage of "if you want something to be done (properly), do it yourself"; the element of control (over quality of work and timescales) is often a barrier to asking for help.

Fran also observed that having to admit to ourselves that we don't have all the answers makes us feel vulnerable and that as we get more experienced at work and at life in general, we find it easier to realise that asking for help is not a weakness, but actually makes us stronger. She said that the act of saying "I need help" can be very powerful and liberating.

Do we feel diminished by asking for help? Are we scared? Or do we simply worry about burdening those we ask for help?

"Sometimes our first and greatest dare is asking for support."
Brené Brown

Research at Columbia University[3] tested a theory, through a number of different studies: that a factor contributing to our reluctance to ask for help is that we underestimate the likelihood that others will help us when we ask. Experiments carried out in a variety of settings found that people underestimated the chances of others agreeing to help them when asked by as much as 50%. A number of factors, according to the findings of this research, influence whether we think we are likely to receive the help we ask for. For example, the research findings cite previous studies showing that we are less likely to ask for larger favours because of the perceived burden or effort the help-giver would incur by helping us.

Given how inaccurate our estimation of the likelihood of us receiving help is, it is perhaps not surprising that we don't ask for help as much as we could. The benefits of asking for help, however, are vast. There is the initial benefit of being able to progress, or achieve what we needed to do, or find an answer we'd been searching for, as a result of obtaining help.

When I was faced with my impending 30th birthday, 11 years ago, I crashed into an early mid-life crisis of sorts. I had imagined that turning 30 would be a positive experience; I would finally be a 'proper adult', respected and treated as an adult by my parents' generation and having made significant strides towards a meaningful career, yet I would still be young enough to have fun and have a lot of life ahead of me still. The reality was different. My job as a teacher wasn't right for me. I was the mother of two very

3. Flynn, Francis J.; Lake, Vanessa K. B. (Jul 2008), 'If you need help, just ask: Underestimating compliance with direct requests for help', Journal of Personality and Social Psychology, Vol 95(1), 128-143

young children and faced the daily conflict between my immeasurable love for them and gratitude for having them in the first place, alongside the difficulties of raising two toddlers with the daily tantrums, the constant need for vigilance and a general level of exhaustion. We were also waiting for a date for Charlie to have the major open heart surgery she needed, so there was a lot of underlying anxiety in my life at the time. This juxtaposition between my previous expectations of turning 30 and the reality of this milestone in my life left me feeling very low and, I have since realised, depressed. Eventually, I reached out to my very good friend Clare, who identified one important practical step for me to take: I needed to change what I did for a living. This marked the beginning of my move into a recruitment career. My husband, Simon, was also immensely supportive during this time. Asking for help was essential to my ability to turn that corner and return to my happy self. Over the years, I have faced many obstacles and I haven't always found it easy to ask for help. Asking for help is a learned skill that doesn't come naturally to many of us. In my early 40s now, I'm getting better at it; let's call it a 'work in progress'. I am, however, often astounded at just how many people, sometimes from the most unexpected sources, are willing to help when I do ask.

Over to you...
Think of a time when you could have benefited from receiving help (of whatever kind) but didn't ask for any.

Describe the situation in writing.

Write down every reason you can think of why you didn't ask for help.

For each reason you have written down, pretend you're your best friend and write down a counter-argument; explain to yourself, in writing, why the reason is not helpful and why you should have asked for help anyway.

Next, make a list of the people who could have helped in that situation.

Is there a situation or problem you're struggling with right now?

If so, repeat the entire exercise, then ask the people on your list to help you.

Finally, write down all the positive outcomes you have experienced as a result of asking for help. Return to this list every time you struggle with something and are tempted to 'go it alone' in future.

Gratitude – Part 2

There is a second benefit to asking for help: the mood-lifting, happiness-enhancing effect of being grateful.

Research into the short- and long-term effects of Positive Psychology[4] methods has shown that gratitude can cause large positive changes (people were happier / less depressed) for one month after carrying out a 'gratitude visit' (participants were instructed to write and personally deliver a letter of gratitude to someone who had been particularly kind to them, but had not been properly thanked previously). In fact, participants in the 'gratitude visit' demonstrated the largest positive changes out of the entire study.

"Be grateful – and you will be happy."
Karl Moore

Gratitude can enhance happiness even when it isn't directed at a person. In chapter one, we looked at the attitudes we choose; the choice to be happy. I mentioned that I chose to be grateful for having my daughters, despite their health circumstances, rather than focus on the negatives. It stands to reason that we will be happier if we focus on what is good in our lives rather than on those aspects of our lives that we wish were different.

4. Seligman, M.E.P., Steen, T.A., Park, N., and Peterson, C. (Jul-Aug 2005), 'Positive Psychology Progress: Empirical Validation of Interventions', American Psychologist, Vol. 60, No. 5, 410 – 421

Entire books[5] have been written on the subject of gratitude and how this enhances happiness and much research has been dedicated to this topic.

When I ask others about their thoughts on happiness and how they stay happy, gratitude is mentioned over and over again.

Jackie has made gratitude part of her daily ritual. She and a very good friend of hers send each other a text message every day with a list of three good things that happened to them that day. This helps them focus on the positives and appreciate what they have. Jackie also makes gratitude declarations every day, e.g. "I love my house, I love my dog etc".

"Gratitude is important to happiness. Studies show that consistently grateful people are happier and more satisfied with their lives; they even feel more physically healthy and spend more time exercising."
Gretchen Rubin

Over to you...
Make a list of everything you are grateful for.

Are there any people you haven't thanked for any acts of kindness towards you?

If so, pick up the phone or go and see them and

5. Thanks! How the New Science of Gratitude Can Make You Happier. Emmons, R. A., Houghton Mifflin, 2007

thank them.

When you get up tomorrow morning, make a point of finding at least one thing to be grateful for. Repeat this every morning; make it part of your morning routine, like brushing your teeth. You may wish to keep a gratitude journal as part of the process.

When you receive good customer service, or someone holds a door open for you in future, make a point of thanking that person and meaning it. Make eye contact while you thank them.

Life does get difficult at times. We face countless obstacles in our personal and professional lives. We encounter things and situations we don't understand. As children, we receive help all the time – from our parents, siblings and teachers. We accept learning as part of our daily lives. There is no reason for this to be different in our adult lives. By asking for, and accepting, help when we need it, we allow ourselves to overcome obstacles and grow; we allow others to feel good about themselves by carrying out the altruistic act of helping someone. When we receive help, we are in a position to be grateful and thus enhance our happiness.

Spaghetti alla Carbonara

Spaghetti alla Carbonara
(Spaghetti with carbonara sauce)

This recipe is one of the big favourites in our house.
Simon and the girls love it! It's simple and quick to
make, yet filling and delicious.

It also holds a special place in my heart and in this
particular chapter of this book, because it was the
first meal I cooked for Simon, when we were still at
University. I asked lots of people for help in my quest
to "win Simon's heart through his stomach":

Most of my friends were on the floor above mine
in our University's halls of residence, so I always
used their kitchen, rather than the one on my floor.
I wanted a room on the same floor as the kitchen
to use as a 'dining room' on this occasion. It was
towards the end of the summer term, after most
people had finished their first year exams, so I asked
a friend to borrow his empty room while he was
away – this allowed me to have a properly set up
'dining table' with candles and a table cloth, rather
than using the desk in my room.

I asked my mum for the recipe.

I asked some friends to act as waitresses and
sous-chefs by bringing in each course at the right
time as well as putting the dessert into the oven while
Simon and I were eating and bringing it in when it
was ready.

Simon had only ever eaten pasta at school before this meal and, unsurprisingly, hadn't enjoyed the over-cooked, soggy offerings he'd had to endure. After he'd tried my authentic Spaghetti alla Carbonara, he was hooked on pasta, hooked on this particular dish and, if he wasn't already beforehand, hooked on me!

Ingredients for 4 people:
- 6 large egg yolks (to avoid waste, why not make meringue with the left-over whites?)
- 70-100g grated pecorino cheese (enough to make a thick paste with the egg yolks - the exact amount will depend on the size of the yolks)
- Plenty of freshly-ground black pepper (to taste, but you do want to see a 'speckled' effect, ideally)
- 200g diced guanciale (if you can't get hold of any, substitute with diced pancetta - I get my guanciale online and dice it myself...it's worth the effort as the taste really is superior as well as authentic)
- A generous dash of olive oil (bear in mind that an Italian 'dash' is quite a large splash!)
- A few drops of vegetable/cooking oil for the pasta cooking water
- Coarse sea salt for pasta cooking water
- Spaghetti for 4 people (approx. 700g)

Method:
Place a large pan / stockpot approximately 3/4 full of water onto the hob and turn the heat on high. While the pasta water comes to the boil, separate the eggs and place the egg yolks in a large serving bowl. Add the grated pecorino cheese and freshly-ground

black pepper to the egg yolks and stir in with a fork. Aim for a thick consistency.

In a frying pan, heat the olive oil and add the diced guanciale, fry until the guanciale fat goes quite transparent and a little bit crispy.

Once the water comes to the boil, add a few drops of oil and a small handful of coarse sea salt. Add the spaghetti when the water is boiling vigorously and push it down with a wooden spoon within a few seconds - as soon as it's soft enough to 'bend' and stir so that all the pasta is in the water and doesn't stick together. Cook the pasta for the indicated time on the pack, but taste it a minute or two before the indicated time to ensure you don't over-cook it. It needs to retain a little bit of 'bite' - the 'al dente' consistency.

Once the spaghetti are cooked, drain them and immediately drop them into the big serving bowl containing the egg yolks, pecorino cheese and black pepper, mixing them with a serving spoon and fork to ensure the pasta is evenly coated in the egg, pecorino & pepper mixture and no 'clumps' form.

Pour on the olive oil and guanciale immediately and mix in. Serve & enjoy.

Buon Appetito!

Pain is a good thing

"Everybody hurts; sometimes, everybody cries"
R.E.M. (Song 'Everybody Hurts')

There is a genetic disorder called 'congenital analgesia', which results in those affected feeling no physical pain. There are other conditions that can cause loss of sensation and, consequently an inability to feel pain: spinal injuries, paralysis, and more. These conditions can be dangerous, because if we don't feel pain, we don't know when we're injured. If you slice through your fingers while cutting vegetables for dinner and you don't notice, you may suffer heavy blood loss and even the onset of infection if there is nobody else around to notice. By the time help comes, it may be too late to save the fingers.

Thus, physical pain is a useful symptom to have. It warns us when something is wrong and requires our immediate and urgent attention. Emotional pain can work much in the same way. Sometimes things are not as they should be, but we push ourselves through; we feel that life must go on, no matter how stressful things are, no matter how unhappy we feel. This is not healthy. It is not sustainable. In fact, there are often resulting physical manifestations when our body decides that enough is enough. Panic and anxiety attacks, depression, heart attacks in more severe cases, where underlying health issues are present.

It is therefore crucial that we learn to recognise when we're in emotional pain or distress, or even better, when we are showing early signs that things aren't as they should be, so that we can make changes.

When **Jackie** hit 'rock bottom' just a few months before I interviewed her for this book, she was desperate. She had made a career change, from being a successful manager in the corporate world, to running her own business, as she'd been feeling that something was missing in her life beforehand. Having taken this bold step towards her own happiness, well-being and fulfilment, she unfortunately also found herself in dire financial circumstances. With no income or client base to start with and no money, the debts started to mount. Loans and credit cards were spiralling out of control. She could see no way out.

Jackie keeps a diary and one day in March 2013, she wrote "I can't see a way out except by killing myself". When she re-read this shortly afterwards, it made her realise just how bad things had got. She needed to do something. So how did she pull herself out and up from the depths of despair?

She realised she was the only person who could do it.

She re-read a spiritual book she had been given previously and that had really helped her see the world differently.

She found a purpose to her life: to help others going through similar situations.

She decided to live in the NOW, to forget about the worries. She learnt to ask herself: Are you happy right now? Do you have enough money for food today? As long as the answer was 'yes', she could get through the day, focus on what was good there and then.

She decided to stop wallowing in self-pity. She took the necessary action to help her situation, knowing deep down that it would be ok. Her strength is her belief in the power of the mind and the universe and in angels. Her beliefs gave her the strength to keep going.

We all go through pain in life. Trying to shield ourselves from all pain would mean numbing ourselves from all the wonderful emotions, too.

"We can't selectively numb emotion. Numb the dark and you numb the light."
Brené Brown

In her book, 'Daring Greatly', Brené Brown writes about vulnerability being "the core of all emotions and feelings".

It is important for us to be vulnerable and to accept the fact that we will feel pain from time to time. This acceptance allows us to deal with situations when they arise. For example, Simon and I have a 'children in hospital' mode of living that we can simply 'switch into' when one of our daughters is in hospital. We slip back into habits; we know that life takes on a different dimension, that time moves at a different pace, that emotions will be fraught and that we just have to get through those times. At those times, we go into 'children in hospital' autopilot and our sole purpose from one day to the next is to put one foot in front of the other and keep going, keep making the decisions we need to make, get through another day. This is our reality, but it is only one of our realities. The rest of the time, we lead our usual lives and put the worries on a shelf. Living in fear of what might be, of the terrible things that might happen, would only stop us from enjoying life.

If I had shielded myself from vulnerability and pain, from the unimaginable ordeals we have been through as a family as a result of Charlie and Hannah's heart conditions, I would also never have been in a position to enjoy every wonderful emotion, every smile, every hug, all the little moments that give me immense happiness as a result of being a mother to my two wonderful daughters. I would perhaps be less courageous in life, more fearful of trying new things. My daughters wouldn't be who they are; they wouldn't be the mature and confident teenagers they are today.

Pain can also serve to immunise us, to some extent, from future pain. It can help us prepare for and face with more strength future traumatic events.

Marc's daughter, Ella, is seven years old and has Cystic Fibrosis. She was diagnosed after birth, from the Guthrie (heel prick) blood test. She was two weeks old when the Consultant phoned Marc's wife to tell her. He was going on holiday and wanted to make sure Ella's parents were informed before he left. Marc was at the gym at the time.

He told me he remembers finding out in the gym changing rooms when his wife 'phoned him, distraught, then driving home in an open top sports car on a glorious sunny day, in a daze, not quite able to take in the reality of what he had just been told. The Doctor had advised them not to look on the internet, but of course they did. They found out the average lifespan was 30 years and Marc still gets very emotional now when he talks of the moment when he sat, holding his two-week old baby daughter, contemplating this fact. He felt heartbroken.

Eventually, they saw the Doctor and discussed everything, found out the facts and, from that point onwards, dealt with the situation.

Two years later, Marc's Mother-in-Law was diagnosed with stomach cancer. It was really bad and they nearly lost her a few times. Marc's wife was asked whether to turn off life support, but she asked the Doctors to give it one more day. Now, five years later, Marc's Mother-in-Law lives on, albeit without a stomach, but with the motivation to enjoy life, her shopping trips and her grandchildren. Marc's wife asked him at the time: "Am I heartless? Why don't I feel worse about this than I do?" They both realised that once they'd experienced the pain they had with Ella, it made everything appear manageable. Not less serious or scary, but they knew they could handle things and deal with the practicalities of it all.

"In order to have hot, you must have cold. In order to have light, you must also have dark. In order to have up, you must have down."
Karl Moore

When Hannah was 10 days old, having had a troublesome winter cold for a few days, she developed bronchiolitis[6]. I had never heard of it before and didn't know what symptoms to look out for. I remember her looking unwell, pulling her tiny little legs up to her chest and looking like she was in pain. I phoned my GP surgery and we agreed it was probably a bit of baby colic and, as the midwife was due to come anyway and see me that afternoon for my ten-day post-natal check-up, that she'd take a look at Hannah. The midwife was delayed with previous appointments and Hannah's condition kept deteriorating. I remember thinking that whatever was wrong with her was very, very serious. She was clammy and grey, her breathing was laboured, she was sleepy and had stopped crying/whimpering. I thought we'd had ten days more than we ever dreamt possible with her, given her prognosis before birth, and that this was it. She was going to die in my arms. I was distraught but also strangely calm and resigned. We'd been lucky - we'd had the opportunity to get to know our daughter. When the midwife rang the doorbell, I greeted her with the words: "Hannah's not well". The midwife took one look at Hannah, who had stopped breathing at that very moment, and said, "I can see that". She took

6. Bronchiolitis is caused by a common viral infection that causes the smallest airways in the lungs (the bronchioles) to become infected and inflamed (swollen). The inflammation reduces the amount of air entering the lungs, making it more difficult to breathe. Source: NHS Choices (www.nhs.uk)

her, placed her gently on the floor, firmly told me to call 999 and proceeded to give Hannah CPR, while intermittently giving calm and competent instructions over the phone to the emergency operator. The ambulance and the police arrived; Hannah started to breathe again and was given oxygen on her way to the hospital. Our wonderful midwife, Angela, came with us, as did Charlie who was a mere toddler at just 23 months old and who'd been golden throughout the entire episode. Angela cancelled all her other appointments and stayed with me, looking after Charlie while I was with Hannah until Simon, my husband, got to the hospital. We will be eternally grateful to Angela, with whom I'm still in contact to this day, for her prompt action. I am also immensely grateful for the serendipitous timing of her arrival at my house that day.

Hannah showed incredible strength throughout her illness. As tiny as she was, she fought off four doctors and nurses who were all trying to insert a cannula[7] into a vein in her hand at the hospital. Despite needing support with her breathing and spending about four weeks in hospital, including some considerable time in paediatric intensive care, she never required full ventilation. Hannah made a full recovery, though she succumbed to every possible chest infection for the following eighteen months or so.

"This is a good sign, having a broken heart. It means we have tried for something."
Elizabeth Gilbert

7. Cannula (noun, plural cannulae / cannulas) a thin tube inserted into a vein or body cavity to administer   medication, drain off fluid, or insert a surgical instrument. Source: http://www.oxforddictionaries.com

When Charlie was twelve years old, on 3rd February 2010, her alarm rang for her to get up for school in the morning. But she didn't wake up. I remember being half asleep, cuddling Hannah who had come into my bed for her early morning pre-breakfast cuddle, and absent-mindedly wondering why I could hear Charlie's alarm clock but no movement. Then again, she had reached that age where getting up in the morning was never a priority or something she did easily! I then heard a strange noise coming from her room and went to investigate. I found my worst nightmare. She was blue, she wasn't breathing and I was unable to feel a pulse. I remember screaming down the stairs for Simon to come up as I couldn't lift her from the top bunk of her bed. Simon placed her on the floor and started doing CPR while I phoned 999 from the phone in our bedroom. Hannah ran between our bedroom and Charlie's, relaying instructions to Simon; within about two minutes the police arrived, closely followed by an ambulance. The paramedics shocked Charlie four times with a defibrillator before they got a faint heartbeat going. I went in the ambulance with Charlie; Simon and Hannah followed in the car. Nobody said much. The mood was sombre.

In hospital, we went through the events chronologically again and again with the doctors and the police officers. The outlook was bleak – Charlie's brain had possibly been deprived of oxygen for approximately ten minutes. Nobody survives that; nobody survives intact. We were asked whether we wanted to let Charlie die peacefully in an adult intensive care unit, or whether we wanted her transferred to a Paediatric Intensive Care Unit, where they would take every possible measure to save her. To save her? Of course that's what we wanted. Lots of calls to hospitals were made and eventually, Leeds was the chosen destination. I phoned my mum and stepdad in Luxembourg and asked them to get on a flight and come say goodbye to their granddaughter. Simon phoned his mum in Birmingham with the same horrific message. I phoned my friend and business partner, Lisa; she came to collect Hannah and look after her. We drove to Leeds in a terrifying daze. We were told yet again that we should prepare for the worst - things were not looking good. We were, ironically, in the same Intensive Care Unit, in the same room, even, that we'd been in with Hannah ten years previously. We tried to stay strong. We wished we could be dying instead of our daughter. We raged at the unfairness of it all. But we maintained hope that, somehow, Charlie might survive. We begged the doctors to keep doing everything they could. And they did. For eight days, they kept Charlie sedated and paralysed and on a cooling blanket, to reduce the swelling in her brain caused by lack of oxygen. We kept talking to her and reading to her. I brought in her iPod - it had previously been mine and it, at that point, only held music by Bob Dylan (Charlie hated this) and Fall Out Boy (Charlie loved them – still does). I kept threatening to play Bob Dylan for her on continuous loop if she didn't get better soon. I kept promising her a pair of the 'Irregular Choice' brand shoes she so desperately wanted if she got better. I implored her not to be a 'sheep' and do what everyone else would do. I told her she was made of stronger stuff than that. Eventually, she showed signs of improvement - enough signs of improvement for the doctors to turn down the sedation and watch for signs of spontaneous breathing. After these encouraging signs appeared, they eventually woke her up completely and turned off the ventilator. She breathed. She opened her eyes and looked at us in complete confusion. She still had the ventilator tube in her trachea, but I asked her: 'Do you want a pair of Irregular Choice shoes when you get out of here?' She beamed at me; her face lit up, and as much as she could with a breathing tube down her throat, she nodded a vigorous and emphatic 'YES!'

Eight days and a few more traumatic complications later, having spent time on the cardiac ward, Charlie received physiotherapy to strengthen her muscles and to teach her to walk, sit and stand again. She was fitted with a new type of defibrillator under her skin; we took her home on Thursday 18th February. By Saturday 20th February, she was strutting her stuff in a brand new pair of 'Irregular Choice' shoes as if she'd been born to walk in heels!

We overcame all these ordeals with the help and support of our friends and family, who were wonderful every step of the way. Going back briefly to the points made in the previous chapter, asking for help in these situations was a crucial step to getting through each day. Simon and I were both diagnosed with PTSD (Post-Traumatic Stress Disorder) after the event and we both received excellent help and support to allow us to move on. Charlie also received support from a psychologist, though having essentially 'slept' through the most traumatic parts, she made a speedy emotional recovery. Hannah didn't want to see a psychologist; she dealt with things in her own way and with a maturity beyond her years.

We are happy again. Charlie is fine. She now loves to shock people with tales of 'the day she died' and loves to rant about people not knowing the difference between a cardiac arrest and a heart attack. In fairness, I do try to explain to her that most teenagers have no need to know the distinction between the two. Life goes on.

Do I wish we hadn't gone through these ordeals as a family? Of course. Does having gone through so much pain make me appreciate all the good times more, though? Absolutely.

In her article 'Escaping the Grip of Emotional Pain' in 'Psychology Today' on 14th January 2013, Dr Leslie Becker-Phelps wrote:

"To be truly happy, you have to know it when you feel it – and when you don't; you must know and let yourself feel that other, not-so-good emotion in order to change it.[…] As counter-intuitive as it might be, labelling and feeling distressing emotions can really help you to feel better in the long run."

Maybe these traumatic events serve as reminders of what is precious in life and what needs nurturing and looking after.

"While suffering is never desirable, that doesn't mean that we can't make use of it, when it is inevitable, to progress humanly and spiritually. Suffering can provide an extraordinary lesson capable of making us aware of the superficiality of many of our daily concerns, of our own fragility, and, above all, of what really counts deep down within us."
Matthieu Ricard

I have faced professional challenges in life that have brought me to tears. I have been bullied at work in the past; I have faced financial difficulties and I've had to make difficult decisions. Things have definitely not always gone the way I hoped they would. Disputes and difficult working relationships are a part of many people's lives. I'm not unique in this.

When these situations arise, I believe that the pain we feel is a strong message saying: 'Get out of this situation!' It's a big megaphone, shouting: 'Make a change'. Change isn't always easy or comfortable. Sometimes we stay in situations because we're worried about upsetting our financial stability. We have mouths to feed, mortgages to pay. At the time of writing this book, I have less financial security and stability than I have ever had in my life. There is a lot of uncertainty and I, like Jackie, have found myself seriously doubting not so long ago whether there was ever going to be a way out. I am convinced, though, that if you believe there is a way out, if you focus on the positives, then you will achieve the results you need, because you're emotionally in the right place to make good decisions and take positive action towards your intended goal.

"What we spend our time and mental energy focusing on can indeed become our reality [...] We become more successful when we are happier and more positive [...] Optimistic salespeople outsell their pessimistic counterparts by 56 percent."
Shaun Achor

I maintain a healthy optimism and positivity that I know will help me achieve my goals. I may not know what my financial future holds, but I know that I am happier now than I've ever been, because I'm doing what I love again.

Accept that just because you chose a certain career path ten years ago it doesn't mean you are obliged to love it still now. You grow, you change. With it, your ambitions, your desires- what lights the fire in your belly that allows you to get up and go to work and love what you do every day - changes. Embrace the change, listen to the pain that tells you to move on and take action.

Over to you...
Think back to a time when you've felt emotional pain.

What was the cause of it?

How did you respond to the pain – what action did you take?

What was the POSITIVE outcome after taking this action?

Write down your answers so you can refer back to them in future, when you find yourself facing difficult challenges. Reading through these answers will serve as a reminder that things do get better and that you can take action to become happy again.

Brodo di Gallina

Brodo di Gallina
(Chicken Stock*)

*Technically, this is Hen Stock. A hen is a female chicken - I thought I'd better specify as someone asked me this recently.

There is something very special about chicken stock. If you're ill or you are in need of an emotional pickup, chicken stock always seems to help. It's warming and comforting, light enough to digest if you're under the weather and it is, somehow, good for the soul.

For me, this has been an essential ingredient to family Christmases throughout my whole life, so it brings back many happy memories every time I smell it cooking in the kitchen. Chicken stock is definitely not just for Christmas, though.

It can be used in so many dishes from soups to sauces to risottos, and tastes delicious on its own, too.

My chicken stock recipe is actually a hen stock with added beef for extra depth of flavour. This is the way I was taught to make it by my mum, who in turn was taught by her mum, my Nonna Wanda. My mum always makes this on Christmas Eve and we enjoy 'Cappelletti in Brodo' - Cappelletti* in broth/stock - as part of our evening meal. It also makes a delicious starter to our Christmas lunch of roast capon with roast potatoes. I've carried on this tradition in our family home here in the U.K.

Brodo di Gallina is also delicious with Capelli d'Angelo (Angel's Hair - very fine pasta) or Pastina (very small pasta shapes). 'Pastina in Brodo' also takes me back to my childhood - many Italian children are still fed this as an early 'weaning' food!

TIP: Essential equipment - a large stockpot

Ingredients
(Makes enough stock to serve Tortellini in Brodo to approximately 8 people, or 4 people over two meals)
- 1 hen, skinned (see http://bit.ly/Skin_Hen for help on skinning a hen) and whole
- 500g (approx.) of stewing beef, in one single piece
- 1-2 onions, depending on size, peeled but left whole
- A selection of root vegetables (e.g. 2-3 carrots
   - scraped clean and topped and tailed; 1 swede
   - peeled and cut into large chunks; 1-2 parsnips -

peeled and topped and tailed)
- Coarse sea salt
- Water

Method

Place the skinned hen and the beef into a large
stockpot and add enough water to ensure both are
covered, but only just (adding too much water will
dilute the flavour). Add a good handful of coarse
sea salt and bring to the boil over a high heat.

Once the water starts boiling, a froth/foam will
start forming on the surface of the water. Remove
this with a fine skimmer (you can simply use a spoon
if you don't have a skimmer). Once you are satisfied
you've removed as much of the froth as you can,
add the onion(s) and root vegetables.

Turn the heat down so the water simmers gently;
cover and leave to cook for approximately two hours
(check after an hour and a half – some of the
vegetables may begin to fall apart, so remove those
that are too soft before they fall to pieces into the
stock). Check for taste as you near the end of
the two hours. You'll know when it's ready as the
taste will be divine and the hen will be close to falling
apart. At this point, add more salt if needed. If you
find that you used too much water and the stock is
a little bland, simply cook it a bit longer with the lid
removed, to reduce it down a little and concentrate
the flavour (careful on salt quantities if you do
this, though, as you may end up with an over-salted
stock).

TIP: If you find you've over-salted it earlier in the process, adding a raw, peeled potato to the cooking process will help absorb some of the excess salt.

Once the stock is ready, carefully lift out the hen and the beef as well as all the vegetables. Now pour the stock through a sieve into a clean stockpot to remove any vegetable debris, ready to use as you wish. If you prefer your stock to be leaner, place it in the fridge overnight, then remove the layer of solidified fat from the top.

If you serve the stock as 'cappelletti in brodo', or with other pasta, add a little sprinkling of freshly-grated parmesan cheese to each individual portion once served for extra-deliciousness.

TIP: Don't waste the beef and hen meat. Tear these up into little strips by hand once they've cooled down enough to handle (but not yet cold) and season with a little olive oil and salt. They're both delicious to eat either warm (not hot) or straight from the fridge, and they make an excellent light meal accompanied by the vegetables, which are also delicious to eat with a drizzle of olive oil; they taste really sweet when cooked in this way.

*Cappelletti (Italian for 'little hats') are similar to tortellini – i.e. filled pasta parcels of sorts, but cappelletti tend to be smaller than tortellini, so are better for serving in brodo' than tortellini. Don't worry if you can't get hold of cappelletti, tortellini will also work (I used tortellini in the photos shown in this recipe).

Pounce on Opportunities

"The follies which a man regrets most, in his life, are those which he didn't commit when he had the opportunity."
Helen Rowland

Are you a person that reacts to life or do you pro-actively 'grab the bull by the horns' and make things happen? It may be an old cliché but sometimes sayings become clichés for a reason. There are things in life that we need to react to, because we wouldn't choose for them to happen; loved ones getting ill, economic crises that force us into unemployment or to instil personal 'austerity measures' or setbacks in business. When it comes to carving out the life we want, however, we could choose to sit back and let things happen to us, but it's unlikely that we'd end up with the desired outcomes. Shouldn't we, then, make our own 'luck', by creating situations likely to lead to our desired outcomes and pouncing on every opportunity that comes our way?

Professor Richard Wiseman carried out a ten-year study into what makes some people exceptionally lucky when others appear to suffer terrible bad luck. He studied 400 people and came to the conclusion that people make their own luck. Furthermore, he found that people can increase their good fortune. In his article 'The Luck Factor' in 'The Skeptical Enquirer' on 1st May 2003, he wrote:

"My research revealed that lucky people generate their own good fortune via four basic principles. They are skilled at creating and noticing chance opportunities, make lucky decisions by listening to their intuition, create selffulfilling prophesies via positive expectations, and adopt a resilient attitude that transforms bad luck into good."

There are likely to be people you admire in life; perhaps these are successful business people or friends, family members, or even public figures that have achieved great success in some way, leaving their mark on the world and making a difference. If you look at the lives of those people, either because you're close enough to them to gather the facts as to how they got to where they are, or by reading their biographies; you're likely to find many instances of opportunities they grabbed with both hands. The Richard Bransons and Lord Sugars of this world haven't always had it easy. They've made mistakes, taken wrong turns and faced many challenges. What makes them different to anybody else? The fundamental difference is that they picked themselves up and tried again when something didn't work out; they realised that to grab opportunities means that sometimes things don't work out, but that failing once – or a hundred times – didn't mean they shouldn't try again.

In 2009, I was a successful recruiter. I had joined a company I loved two years previously, having found a synergy between mine and the business owner's values. In an environment where I had been allowed to grow, to develop ideas and take ownership of projects and turn those ideas into reality, I had spent those two years developing and growing into my role, recruiting and training new team members and progressing into the roles, firstly, of Senior Recruitment Consultant and then Business Operations Manager.

Then, I started hearing two little words on the news: 'credit crunch'. I wasn't even sure what those two words meant at first. People were asking me whether the 'credit crunch' had affected the recruitment business. It hadn't. Gradually, though, fewer enquiries came into the business; sales calls and other business development activities seemed to fall on deaf ears; clients attempted to negotiate lower and lower fees and placements fell through at the eleventh hour. Something was happening. As the year progressed, 'credit crunch' was no longer the 'phrase du jour'. 'Recession' and 'economic crisis' - these words were all over the media. Things got difficult; morale in the office was low. As the most senior member of the team, reporting directly to the business owner, I found myself in more and more meetings, reviewing dire-looking financials and making very difficult decisions regarding people's lives. People I had recruited and trained, and whose progression and development I'd watched with pride and affection - people I called my friends. Redundancies were inevitable. The team shrank and, with a smaller team rattling around in a big office and as making ends meet became a daily struggle, morale spiralled further, hitting an all-time low.

I felt very strongly that this was a business I believed in, that we still had a lot to accomplish and that it wasn't time to give up yet. I had already been working in the business as though I was a part of it, as more than an employee. I therefore saw an opportunity: to help the business survive and eventually grow again and an opportunity for my personal development. I discussed with my Managing Director the possibility that I could buy shares in the business, in order to inject much-needed cash. I didn't have any cash myself, so I had some difficult conversations with my mum. It wasn't an easy process but we got there. I borrowed money from my mother and bought shares in the business. The business lived to see another day; we were able to keep paying people a little longer. There was hope for the future.

The economy continued to provide challenges every day. Things weren't easy and the financials were still a struggle. In 2010, I bought more shares in the business, which made me a 50% shareholder and joint Managing Director in the business I loved and believed in. Nobody could have predicted how long the economic crisis would continue for. I am an eternal optimist, so I ploughed on regardless. Things have been a struggle, but eventually we turned the business around from a financial loss to a healthy profit.

I have learnt more in the last four years than I could ever have hoped to learn from any academic course. I have a business and management degree from the highly respected Management School at the University of Bradford and although having that background gave me some very useful theoretical foundations to my life in business, actually going through the most challenging, most difficult economic times my generation has lived through has been the best learning experience I could have had. If I hadn't grabbed the initial opportunity to buy shares in the business, I wouldn't have opened my mind up to the possibility of self-employment; I wouldn't have set up my sole trader business in social media marketing. I wouldn't have ever dreamt of setting up my own food business. I wouldn't have embarked on a speaking career and started writing a book. Through personal and financial challenges, I have learnt new skills and found a new resourcefulness I didn't realise I possessed. I have now sold my shares back to my business partner so that I can focus on my new career.

My life has changed in ways I never imagined and I am happier than ever before. I still get scared, but I am excited about the world of possibilities ahead of me.

"It is such a challenge to see the opportunities in changing situations, whether it's a change in our role at work or something in our home life, because change inevitably seems to put us outside of our comfort zone. [...] But there eventually came a turning point in the journey when I realised that the comfort zone seemed to be shifting to where I was."
Debra Searle

Sometimes the opportunities we find before us are of a more personal nature. My parents separated when I was nine years old. For a few years I saw my father regularly, but he then said and did some things that I found deeply upsetting. At the age of fourteen, I decided not to see him anymore. I told him and carried on living my life; eventually, my father moved away from Luxembourg - where I lived at the time - to Brussels. Our paths didn't cross and I had no desire to rekindle the relationship. I did, however, have a niggling doubt over the years. It is inevitable that everyone dies, sooner or later, the natural order that parents die before their children. I therefore had this worry in the back of my mind: how would I feel once my father died, knowing I'd never made a move towards some kind of relationship with him? Would I forever live with regret?

A few years ago, an opportunity presented itself to me. I had arranged to go to Sardinia with Simon, Charlie and Hannah, to stay at my cousin's holiday home, where I'd spent many happy summers as a child. I was looking forward to a wonderful holiday catching up with extended family and enjoying with my own family the most beautiful sea, in my opinion, in the world. I was eagerly anticipating creating new memories and giving my daughters the opportunity to experience the place that had given me so many wonderful childhood summers. I hadn't been back to Sardinia for approximately fourteen years and I was almost bursting with anticipation.

My cousin then 'phoned and told me that she'd found out my father was going to be there at the very same time we were planning to go. He was going to be there with his daughters from his second marriage - two girls roughly the same ages as my own children. It was a little bit of a shock, to say the least. My cousin explained she would fully understand if we wanted to change our plans. I must admit, I considered it. I wasn't sure whether I was ready to face my father and for him to meet my daughters. They already had a grandfather - my mother's second husband; my stepfather has been in my life since I was around thirteen years old. I then decided to look upon this as an opportunity: the chance to remove any doubts or regrets about the choices I had made. I saw my father and behaved in a wholly civilised manner towards him. We even had meals and sight-seeing days together. I spent time with my younger sisters and they had great fun with Charlie and Hannah. My father could have taken the opportunity to keep the relationship going after he had seen me, but he didn't. I still have no desire to have my father in my life, but I now have no regrets. I have seen him again and I have made my peace with my feelings towards him. I have established that he seems to have no more interest in having me in his life than I have in having him in mine. I hope he lives a long and healthy life. When nature takes over and he eventually dies, I now know I won't have any regrets about lost years or opportunities. Our paths simply went a different way and that's okay.

"The only place you can be is here; make the most of it, don't waste the opportunity to make the best of it."
Nigel Risner

Despite his daughter's cystic fibrosis, and even though he may not have as many material possessions as some, Marc considers himself to have a charmed life and to be exceptionally lucky. If an opportunity presents itself, he grabs it. His mum used to say that he could 'fall into a pile of horse manure and come out smelling of roses'. Once, a double-glazing salesman came to his door and ended up buying lilies from Marc's pond instead!

In her 'Happiness Weekly' blog, Sarah Webb wrote on 4th May 2013:

"A lot of people classify 'opportunists' – particularly in the workplace – as manipulative, and it brings with it many negative connotations. Opportunism is the most misunderstood yet highest-impact approach to decision-making. What is wrong with making the best of a situation you find yourself in?"

In 'The Happiness Advantage', Shaun Achor references research[8] showing that 69% of students attributed career decisions on chance encounters. Achor stipulates that 'the difference between people who capitalize on their chances and those who watch them pass by (or miss them entirely) is all a matter of focus.' He goes on to state that 'we can train our brains to let in these messages that make us more adaptive, more creative and more motivated – messages that allow us to spot and pounce on more opportunities at work and at play'.

The opportunities we pounce on don't necessarily have to be huge life-changing ones in order to impact on our happiness. Often it is the little opportunities in life that make all the difference. For example, how do you view a long car journey? Is it a chore, an inconvenience, a waste of time? Or is it an opportunity to spend some quiet time contemplating something you need to find an answer or solution to? Or perhaps it's an opportunity to turn your favourite music up loud and sing along without fear of your children telling you to 'shut up, you can't sing' (in my

8. Bright, J.E., Pryor, R.G.I., Harpham, L., (2005) 'The role of chance events in career decision-making', Journal of Vocational Behavior, 66, 561-576,

case, they're right, so all the more reason to make the most of those car journeys on my own). A train journey is a great opportunity to read a few chapters of your favourite book. Forgetting to take your packed lunch to work with you could be the perfect excuse, i.e. opportunity, to leave the office at lunchtime and catch up with some friends over a bite to eat.

It isn't always easy to see opportunities hidden amidst the challenges in our lives. Sometimes the present feels so bleak, terrifying and hopeless, that we cannot see beyond our current circumstances. Sometimes we just have to put one foot in front of the other and keep going, hoping that there will be 'light at the end of the tunnel'. The key is to train our brains to spot more opportunities and to run towards that light when we see it; to believe that a tiny spot of light is worth heading towards when we are surrounded by bleak darkness, that a little flicker of brightness will allow us to see things more clearly and to make informed decisions.

'Getting it right' isn't always the goal. We learn more from our mistakes than we ever will from doing everything right and playing it safe. Pouncing on opportunities requires taking risks, but risks – professional, emotional or financial – can lead to great rewards.

Over to you...
Think back to some of the successes you have enjoyed in your life. Were any of them due to chance encounters? Which opportunities did you grab?

Make a note of the opportunities you have grabbed and the results of doing so.

Make a conscious effort to look for opportunities in every situation. Train your brain to spot opportunities and grab them with both hands.

Bruschetta

Bruschetta
(Bruschetta = Italian Garlic Bread)

I have chosen bruschetta as the recipe for this chapter, because it is the ultimate opportunistic food. To take a humble piece of bread – possibly even slightly stale – and turn it into the perfect starter to a meal, or a fantastic snack to enjoy with friends and family, embodies the philosophy of pouncing on opportunities.

Bruschetta is one of those foods that instantly puts me in a good mood and transports me back to so many summers spent in Italy over the course of my life.

Basic bruschetta is simply barbecued bread slices rubbed with whole cloves of garlic and served with a drizzle of olive oil and a pinch of salt. It couldn't be simpler.

The picture shows a very common variation: Tomato bruschetta.

Ingredients
- Slices of fairly firm/rustic bread (typically you'd use 'Pane Casareccio' but a good ciabatta or similar firm bread will work)
- Whole garlic cloves, peeled
- Extra virgin olive oil
- Sea salt

- Fresh tomatoes, chopped into small pieces
- Fresh basil, roughly chopped

Method

Start by making the tomato topping for the bruschette (Italian lesson: bruschette = plural of bruschetta). Chop the tomatoes into small pieces and place into a bowl, along with a generous amount of roughly chopped basil leaves. Add a generous amount of extra virgin olive oil (you will need plenty of juices to soak into the bread) and season with salt, to taste. Leave to stand until needed (try to make this at least 15 minutes before you toast/barbecue your bread slices).

Slice the bread into 2cm thick slices and toast on a barbecue or under a grill (barbecued tastes nicer).

Once the bread slices are toasted, rub a raw, peeled garlic clove over each slice (how much you rub on depends on how strong you want the garlic flavour to be) and immediately top with a generous amount of the previously seasoned tomatoes, ensuring each slice of bread gets plenty of tomato/olive oil 'juice'.

Serve immediately before the bread goes too soggy.

I guarantee this will put a smile on your face, but beware...don't eat this the day before an important business meeting or a date, as the raw garlic does tend to linger on the breath for a while!

Imagine...

"Dreams come true; without that possibility nature would not incite us to have them."
John Updike

When we were children, the possibilities before us were limitless. A young child sees only possibilities, not obstacles. If young children allowed self-doubt to take over, human beings would never learn to sit, stand and walk. Toddlers fall over, pick themselves up and start again. They see an object out of their reach and don't think: 'I can't get that'; they think 'how can I get that?', then they go for it. If we allow ourselves to view the world and the endless possibilities before us in a childlike way, we open up our minds to opportunities and vast achievements.

Hannah talks about her future in terms of 'when I am a paediatric cardio-thoracic surgeon' and Charlie talks about 'when I study history at Cambridge' and 'when I am a famous author'. The possibility of failure doesn't even enter their minds. Are they naïve? Maybe, but if you don't dream or shoot for the stars, you exclude from the outset the possibility of ever reaching them.

In his article 'Imagination: Powers and Perils' for Raritan Journal on 1st October 2012, Mark Edmundson stated that imagination can 'be a way of making contact with real possibilities of an individual and a collective sort'. He added that 'a person without imagination has no real capacity to envision a more humane and rich future and then try to create it. He'll be unequipped to understand how his life could be turned into something better than it is.'

Your dreams may change, your outcomes may not be those that you initially imagined, but that doesn't ultimately matter.

When I was at school and had decisions to make about university, only one thing was certain. There was no university in Luxembourg. I therefore needed to move to a different country. I had a few options: I could study in France, Italy, Germany or the U.K. The U.K. was the furthest away from home and a country where I had no connections or support network whatsoever. I decided, however, that the U.K. was a country where the university system was most closely aligned to the way I wanted to learn and study. My mother and I attended lots of open days in one of the coldest, most gruelling winters we'd had for a while. We got snowed in and we were almost stuck in Bradford. It was cold, wet and culturally different to everything I knew. I had a dream of becoming a 'Big Manager' though - a vision of myself in the future. I had ambitions and plans and none of these inconveniences were going to stand in my way. I had no 'Plan B'. Not getting accepted by a U.K. university and not getting my first choice of university - neither were outcomes I considered. The University of Bradford was my first choice and that's how I found myself packing suitcases to move away from home for my first term and ten weeks in Bradford, full of excitement, eager anticipation and dread in equal measures, in September 1990.

Moving to Bradford was a culture shock: I was used to hearing lots of languages around me, yet suddenly I was surrounded by people speaking English. I had been at the same school since kindergarten (nursery) and now I had to make completely new friends. I had never even heard of 'having a curry'; I had no idea what I'd been missing out on for the first eighteen years of my life! I was home-sick at first, of course, and had to adjust. I am so delighted to have taken the plunge, though because I had an absolute blast at university. I enjoyed studying for my Business and Management degree. I made lifelong friends and met the love of my life, Simon. My original plan had been to study in the U.K. then do an MBA at Harvard (USA), and eventually move to Italy. We have an Italian holiday every year and when we get back home to the U.K., I do feel homesick all over again for a little while, for the weather, the food and the language. I do miss it, even though I never lived in Italy in the first place (unless I count the first two years of my life). What I have now, however - the reality - is so much better than what I imagined and dreamt of. I have a wonderful family and great friends. I am happy.

"Things don't have to go to plan to work out well."
Debra Searle

I started a food blog a couple of years ago. The reason behind this, beyond my passion for food and cooking and to share this passion with others, was that I had taken part in a cookery TV show (Britain's Best Dish) as a contestant, thoroughly enjoying the experience. I wanted to find a way to showcase my cooking skills and open up more opportunities for future TV work related to food. In short, I wanted to become the next 'Nigella'!

I allowed myself to daydream and to imagine limitless possibilities. I allowed myself to envisage a future within which a TV producer might 'spot' one of my recipe videos on YouTube or where my blog would become a hugely successful food platform, with a loyal following that would eventually buy my cookbooks when I published them. I decided to push away the little voice that said: 'You're in your late thirties; you've missed that boat. Focus on your career instead. Don't be silly.' I replaced it with a little voice that said, 'What do you have to lose?' I decided to continue to dream big but to enjoy the journey, regardless of the outcome. I started writing my blog and posting videos on YouTube as though I was already famous with a huge following; an eager public already looking forward to my next instalment. I'm not the next Nigella (yet!); I'm not even on TV. I haven't written a cookbook (yet!). I have immense fun creating recipes and sharing recipes with my growing number of followers. Perhaps I wouldn't be writing this book right now, with recipes and photographs, if it wasn't for my blogging journey.

Imagining and dreaming don't have to be restricted to major life decisions and future ambitions. I believe that daydreaming can allow your subconscious to find ideas and solutions by kick-starting the thinking process and opening up your imagination to more possibilities. If you have a problem, allowing yourself to daydream and imagine seemingly wildly unlikely scenarios and outcomes can be a great way to find solutions. Brainstorming and mind-mapping work on this very principle. It's always easier to discard ideas if you have too many than it is to try and envisage a solution when you feel there are no options available to you. There are always options; there is always more than one possible outcome to any situation. You just need to open up your mind to the possibilities.

Athletes are often quoted to be using visualisation techniques, where they visualise themselves winning. Seeing the desired outcome play out like a film in their minds - until they have done it so much that when they start the race/competition, winning is the only outcome they can envisage, because they have already experienced it - is a very powerful technique, one which you can use to achieve your desired outcomes.

In her book, 'The Journey', Debra Searle talks about visualisation of negative outcomes, too. She writes about the terror of what lay ahead of her on her solo rowing journey across the Atlantic Ocean – such as the fear of sharks and storms, and all the other dangers she faced. She talks about how she used vivid visualisation of possible future scenarios that scared her in order to plan ways to overcome each of those situations. She 'played the movie' in her head over and over again so that when she did face dangerous storms, for example, she could just tell herself to 'play the movie' and she'd know what to do to stay safe.

This can be a very powerful technique to give you the confidence to overcome difficult situations when you know you are going to hit obstacles on your personal journey. Acknowledging that these obstacles will occur and envisaging worst case scenarios in a practical way, by visualising how you would deal with those scenarios, allows you to tackle those situations when they do arise. You're then not caught by surprise and left scrabbling for solutions in a blind panic; you'll already know what to do. Because you'll have visualised the scenario, you can handle it with confidence and experience.

In 'The How of Happiness', Sonja Lyubomirsky takes this further and talks about the difference between extrinsic and intrinsic goals:

"There is persuasive evidence that following your dreams is a critical ingredient of happiness. But does it matter what that dream is and how you follow it? Indeed, it does. It turns out that the type of goal or 'valued life task' that you pursue determines whether the pursuit will make you happy. [...] Working towards goals that are personally involving and rewarding to you is more likely to bring you happiness than working towards goals that are not freely chosen."

Thus, merely working towards objectives set by an employer, for example, will not necessarily make you happy. This is where allowing your imagination to run free and allowing yourself to daydream comes into its own. Regardless of what you are doing in life and whether your dreams are for your professional future or your personal life, having dreams of your own (no matter how far-fetched) and then pursuing them - taking actions to turn them into reality - will majorly contribute to your fundamental happiness.

Over to you...
Spend some time imagining what you want to achieve. Dream big, dream bold, dream multi-dimensionally.

Keep a record. Write it in a diary, keep a blog, have a 'dream board' (you can even use Pinterest as a 'dream board' mechanism to keep a visual record of your dreams and ambitions).

Imagine yourself having achieved your desired outcome. What are you doing? What do you look like? What can you hear, see, smell, touch? Brainstorm liberally; set yourself no limits. Build on your dream over time. Don't be afraid to make changes as time goes on, but always dream big.

Share your dreams with those closest to you. By letting other people in on your plans, you make yourself accountable and will allow others to help you achieve your big dreams.

Make a list of what you need to do in order to achieve your dream, in small, manageable steps, then act on each of those steps.

What do you have to lose?

Pea and Asparagus Soup

Pea and Asparagus Soup

This is one of my own original recipes, rather than an Italian 'classic'.

This dish is very close to my heart and intrinsically linked to the value of letting your imagination run wild. This is possibly the first of my own creations that I shared with a wider audience than just my own family. I took it to work and colleagues tried it, giving me fantastic feedback. It was one of the first recipes to go into my food blog.

This recipe is also a great example of what you can achieve when you allow your imagination to roam free. I have seen many soup combinations on supermarket shelves, in recipe books and websites, but when I created this soup a few years ago, I hadn't seen asparagus and peas put together in a soup. I don't know where the idea originally came from – it was one of those 'it popped into my mind' outcomes that occur once you allow your imagination free rein. It is the result of allowing your mind to be creative without the boundaries we impose on ourselves as we grow up. It is what happens when you allow yourself to be childlike in your dreams.

It is simple, tasty, quick to make and requires very little effort. When you are busy dreaming big and taking action to make your dreams come true, it's great to have simple recipes to hand that don't require too much time or effort to accomplish. This recipe also makes me happy because it's so vividly green. Food that looks bright and colourful always puts a smile on my face and I hope it will have the same effect on you.

Ingredients
- 2 big bunches of fresh asparagus spears (approx. 750g)
- 1 medium bag (900g) of frozen peas or petits pois
- Boiling water
- 2 x stock cubes (I personally like using Knorr Chicken Stockpots, but any chicken or - if feeding vegetarians - vegetable stock cubes will work)
- Salt, to taste
- Freshly ground nutmeg, to taste
- 40g fresh butter

Method
Chop the asparagus spears into approximately 1cm lengths, keeping the pointy ends, plus one or two extra cuts, to use separately later.

Melt 30g of butter in a medium/large stockpot, then add the bulk of the chopped asparagus (but NOT the ends you've kept to one side) and turn the heat up. Add salt and stir.

After about a minute or so, add the frozen peas; stir, and grate in a sprinkling of fresh nutmeg.

Cover with boiling water (to about 1cm above the solid ingredients).

Add stock cubes/pots.

Bring to a rolling boil until the peas and asparagus are cooked (approx. 5 mins); the softer the peas, the smoother the soup - so it's down to personal preference how long you cook it for. Taste the stock during the cooking process and add either salt or another stock cube/pot (or part of one) if it requires more seasoning.

Turn the heat off and leave it to cool for a few minutes, then process in a food blender (I find it easiest to use a hand blender that you can simply place into the pan; if you use a jug-style blender while the soup is still hot, make sure you leave the central section of the lid open, covering with a folded tea-towel so that steam can escape without the lid flying off).

In a separate pan, fry off the asparagus tips you previously kept aside in the remaining butter, and season with salt (to taste). They need to be cooked but still crunchy, so you only need to fry them for 1-2 minutes.

Stir the fried asparagus tips into the soup.

Next!

"The universe is truly in love with its task of fashioning whatever is next to be."
Marcus Aurelius

We all make mistakes. Some of the most successful business people in the world have made a lot of mistakes along the way; some of those mistakes have bankrupted them on occasion. One such example would be Peter Jones, CBE, known by the general public mostly for his long-standing role as a 'Dragon Investor' on the BBC's 'Dragon's Den'. He bankrupted himself at 28, but look at him now. When you read the autobiographies of great entrepreneurs and other big achievers in life, the one thing that really stands out is that they learn from their mistakes and move on. They don't give up.

After I completed my business degree, I assessed my options. My degree was good, especially in light of me having obtained it at a British university as a non-Brit, but it wasn't earth-shatteringly great. It was a 2(ii) Hons degree. I had enjoyed myself at university and had perhaps not always dedicated as much time to studying as I could have. This meant that it was virtually impossible for me to compete for the one or two marketing positions (and as just one of thousands of applicants) offered to graduates by each of the blue chip companies during the recruitment 'milk round'. I needed to reassess my options. By then, I had been in a relationship with Simon for some time and we both knew we wanted a life together. He was part-way through completing a five-year combined

BEng/MEng (Bachelor of Engineering / Master of Engineering) degree and was heading for top-level results. He stood a very good chance of obtaining a great job with a great company and, due to the nature of his work as a chemical engineer, there were only going to be so many locations he could work in. A chemical plant was prerequisite; these tend to be in specific locations, usually near a body of water.

I realised that I had other options: there are schools everywhere. I could teach, and this would allow me to follow Simon wherever he ended up working. I wanted to be sure that teaching was for me, so I spent some time in my final year at university working as a volunteer in a local school in Bradford. I loved the experience. I also did a four-week 'TEFLA' (Teaching English as a Foreign Language to Adults) course at Leeds Metropolitan University and absolutely loved every minute of it. This proved useful beyond its value as an assessment tool, regarding my suitability to becoming a teacher, as I ended up spending two very happy summers teaching English to foreign students in Harrogate. I subsequently enrolled in a PGCE (Post-Graduate Certificate in Education) degree at Huddersfield University. It was a year of gruelling hard work and sleep deprivation, fitting in many teaching hours and associated planning and marking, along with essay writing and providing evidence of my progress, but I thoroughly enjoyed the year.

It turned out, however, that many schools wanted business studies teachers to have business experience, so it was quite a few years after I qualified that I finally ended up as a 'proper' teacher in a secondary school. Here came a shock: I had been in relatively pleasant schools during my teacher training placements. I also hadn't faced the same pressures that actual teachers face every day in their jobs. I had a very difficult time, not helped by the fact that barely two weeks into my first job, we were called in by Birmingham Children's Hospital for Hannah's long-awaited open heart surgery, and I ended up having the entire first half-term off work. I survived my first year of teaching – and it really did feel like survival – and as I had been on a one-year contract, found it relatively easy to look for a new teaching position and move on. I found my second year even more troublesome. I felt that I was failing my students on a daily basis because I couldn't control the behaviour of the few in order to teach the many. I realised there were other people better equipped than I was to do the job and I absolutely admire those that succeed in this extremely challenging and often demoralising profession. It is a calling and, I came to realise, it wasn't my calling. Making the decision to move on was painful. I wasn't sure about my options. In the chapter 'Asking for Help', I mentioned how my great friend, Clare, helped me evaluate my career options and make a move into recruitment. With her help, I moved on. I experienced a new phase of my life; I learnt new skills. Out of this difficult and, at times, painful experience, I emerged full of enthusiasm for my new career and with new ambitions and goals in my professional life. It was an exciting time again.

Moving on to the next thing has the power to do this. Everyone can put negative experiences behind them and start again. We're never too old to learn new skills and it's never too late to start a new chapter in our lives.

My teaching experience has served me well over the

years. I learnt a lot about behaviour management that, in a less extreme setting as a parent of two rather than a teacher of large groups of over thirty students at a time, I was able to put into practice with my own daughters to defuse major temper tantrums and avoid escalation of conflict. Of course, I'm only human, so from time to time I forget all the great pedagogic tools I learnt. Having been a teacher hasn't turned me into the perfect parent, but I believe I'm a better parent thanks to my teaching experience. Now, I do a lot of work as a social media marketing trainer and my experience as a teacher, in terms of planning lesson content and people's learning styles, is proving to be very handy indeed.

Moving on and learning from experiences is widely used as a development tool. It also features in 'competency-based' job interviews. The STAR 'competency-based' interview technique, for example, stands for 'Situation – Task – Activity – Result'. The 'Result' component often includes an element of review/learning outcomes. Typically, an interviewer would ask you to talk about a situation you faced at work that would demonstrate a particular 'soft skill', for example: 'organisational skill'. You would start by talking about the situation, describing the lead-up to it and its context. Then, you would talk about the tasks that were expected of you in that situation, followed by the activities you actually carried out. Finally, you would describe the result, or outcome. As part of this process, a good interviewer using 'competency-based' interview techniques would also ask you to assess what went well and what didn't go so well, what you learnt from the experience and what you might do differently in a similar situation next time. Incidentally, you can answer interview questions using the STAR technique even if you're not in a structured, 'competency-based' interview by simply applying the structure to your answer.

I once received some great sales training using the 'Sandler Technique', where the trainer used a fantastic quote. I even put it up on the wall next to my desk as a reminder to move on when yet another sales call resulted in a rejection. I cannot, unfortunately, trace the exact origin of the quote, though it appears to have been initially used by sales trainer John Boe in 2008, as the heading to an article in 'Senior Market Advisor' Magazine. I know it has since been famously used by the character Neville Wilshire (Nev) in the BBC3 series 'The Call Centre':

"Some will, some won't. So what? … Next!"

This quote is relevant in all aspects of life. Some people will like you, some won't. So what? Stop trying to please everyone and move on. Some things will go well in your life, some won't. So what? Move on to the next chapter. Some of your hard work will be rewarded, some won't. So what? Don't let it stop you from trying. Move on to the next thing. Try again.

"If what you do isn't creating the desired result, you have still created a result. Use the feedback you get to explore what you can do differently to get the outcome you want. Ask yourself 'What can I learn from this?' and 'What can I do differently?' Focus on solutions and what else is possible, rather than problems. Failure exists only

as a state of mind – a perception."
David Molden & Pat Hutchinson

Sometimes we need to move on from circumstances we find ourselves in for reasons beyond our control. Life sometimes throws things at us that we'd rather not face. Things don't always go to plan and sometimes people hurt or disappoint us. We can choose to remain trapped in the negative circle of our emotions when these things happen, or put these situations and circumstances behind us once they are over and as we move on to the next stage of our lives. If we look carefully, we may even find that there is some good or a lesson to be learnt from each situation we leave behind.

It is most difficult to move on when we have been deeply wounded, emotionally, by someone we cared about. It is easy to harbour resentment, to hold on to the negative emotion and to let that fuel our actions. Moving on requires a certain amount of determination in itself. Moving on can sometimes feel like a self-betrayal. I'm not a particularly religious person so I personally don't subscribe to the notion of forgiveness as a prerequisite to inner peace or the ability to move on. I know some people do and find it very useful, so you may want to try forgiving those that have caused you pain and you may well find it helps you. I do know, though, that anger can fester and grow if it is allowed to. It can go as far as to cause physical symptoms of illness because of all the tension it builds inside us. Letting go of anger and hurt and the situation that caused these emotions in the first place is therefore essential to our well-being. Sometimes this means you need to distance yourself from people or situations that cause you emotional pain in order to allow yourself to move on. This was the choice I referred to earlier in this book when, at the age of fourteen, I told my father I didn't want him in my life. It is also a choice I made around the same age when my boyfriend and my then best friend cheated on me with each other; I moved away from the relationship and the friendship and returned to previous friends I knew I could trust and that I have retained as lifelong friends since.

Choosing not to put yourself in situations that have caused you harm is a natural self-preservation mechanism. It embodies the 'Some will, some won't. So what?...Next!' philosophy.

"Letting go doesn't mean you 'forgive' [...] it just means that you release the negative emotion inside of you."
Karl Moore

My eldest daughter, Charlie, demonstrated a darkly humorous example of the 'Next!' philosophy when we lost our dog, Sadie May, last year. Sadie May was a week away from her sixteenth birthday and had had a very good life, so the best thing we could have hoped for happened when the time came for her to die. She had a massive stroke and we had to take her to a veterinarian so she could be put to sleep. We knew she couldn't have lived forever and had been dreading the moment her life came to an end. We were relieved she hadn't suffered any protracted illness nor suffered from old age and had simply gone when her time came, very suddenly. The four of us

went to the vet's surgery together and lovingly said goodbye to Sadie May. No sooner had our beloved dog's heart stopped beating, than Charlie said: "Now can I have a turtle?"
This certainly broke the sombre spirit of the moment as we just had to laugh! It may seem callous, in retrospect, but I believe that at the tender age of fourteen, Charlie understood fundamentally and subconsciously that Sadie May had had her time with us - that her loss, while very sad for all of us, was not tragic but part of the natural order of things, and that we needed to move on. 'Next!', so to speak. Charlie is still attempting to coax us into getting her a turtle, terrapin or tortoise of some description; we keep reiterating that it's not going to happen!

In her 'Psychology Today' article 'Escaping the grip of emotional pain', Dr Leslie Becker-Phelps talks of the need to move on:
'Move on. After feeling your emotions and treating them with compassion, it is time to refocus on other things – preferably situations, activities, or interactions that feel good.'

Over to you...
Think back to a situation you have moved on from.
What was the situation? Why did you need to move on? Was it difficult to do?

Write down what you have learnt from the experience. Make a note of the positives you took from the situation. Then use those notes to remind you, when facing difficult situations in future, that you CAN move on and that you may even find positives to take with you into the future, even if it seems impossible at the time.

If you are currently facing a difficult situation or feeling negative/painful emotions that you suspect you need to put behind you, make a list of all the reasons why you feel you need to move on and reflect on what your life might look and feel like once you have done this. Then write down all the steps you think you will need to take in order to move on and take the steps, one at a time.

Ossobuco di Nonna Wanda

Ossobuco di Nonna Wanda
(Nonna Wanda's Ossobuco Recipe)

This is my late grandmother's version of 'Ossobuco alla Milanese' (Ossobuco Milanese Style).

Ossobuco are veal shanks, famous for their tender meat and the delicious bone marrow inside the 'buco' – the hole – in the bone. (Osso = bone; buco = hole).

This is one of my all-time favourite recipes. My 'Nonna Wanda' (Grandma Wanda, on my mother's side) used to cook this for me as a special treat, often making sure it was the first meal she cooked for me whenever I arrived in Rome. My aunt is now carrying on the tradition and cooks this for me when I visit.

I miss my grandmother an awful lot and she will always be part of many happy childhood memories. I also understand it's normal for our grandparents to die before us; Nonna Wanda had reached a good age before she died. My children were able to meet her on more than one occasion and she was able to delight in her great-grandchildren. We are now all able to move on in life, remembering her fondly and taking with us many happy memories. This recipe is one such memory. It also happens to be one of the most delicious meats on this planet!

Ingredients (for 4 people)
• 4 veal ossobuco pieces (approx. 0.8–1.2kg in total)

- Butter, generous amount, approx 70-100g
- Flour, enough to give the meat a generous coating
- Stock, you can use vegetable or chicken stock, nothing that would overpower the delicate taste of the veal ossobuco. I used home-made chicken stock on this occasion. You will need just enough to cover the ossobuco pieces in the pan.
- Flat-leaf parsley, a good handful, coarsely chopped
- Lemon rind, finely-grated, from one large lemon
- Anchovy paste, a small amount, approximately 1tsp

Method

Each piece of ossobuco has a thin fat layer that holds it together in its characteristic shape. Cut through this in a few places to stop the ossobuco pieces curling up during cooking, then coat each piece generously in plain white flour.

Heat the butter in a deep sauté pan or shallow casserole dish. As soon as it starts to sizzle, add the ossobuco pieces and seal on both sides.

Pour enough hot stock over the pieces of meat to just cover them. Bring to the boil, then cover with a lid and reduce the heat, leaving them to simmer for 30-45 minutes, until the meat is tender and the marrow starts to seep out of the bone (don't cook it so long that it seeps out - one of the great things about this dish is sucking the marrow from the hole in the bone).

While the meat is cooking, coarsely chop the flat-leaf

parsley and grate the zest of one large lemon. Mix this with the anchovy paste.

Once the meat is cooked, add the parsley, lemon and anchovy paste to the pan and gently stir (or simply turn over the pieces of ossobuco); replace the lid and simmer for a further couple of minutes.

Serve immediately with mashed potato, pouring a generous amount of the velvety sauce over the meat and potatoes. My grandmother always used to make little wells in the mashed potato with the back of a spoon before filling them with sauce. Enjoy the delicious meat, then pick up the bone and suck out the rich marrow!

Energy

"Happiness consists in activity. It is running steam, not a stagnant pool."
John Mason Good

Energy can have different meanings or connotations for people. It can invoke images of physical activity, or of invisible threads of connection between people and objects in the universe. Energy can signify effort. Energy is what we need to heat and light our homes, to power our cars and computers and to cook our food.

Being fundamentally happy can require some energy input on our part; making time and space for all those little happiness ingredients sometimes means we have to put in some effort in order to be happy.

When I was a teacher, I used to use an alphabet exercise that required students to stand up and put their left arm, their right arm or both arms up for certain letters, while they recited the alphabet out loud. It was a great energiser to use at the start of an afternoon session when they'd be typically more sluggish and less alert, or first thing in the morning when some of them looked like they hadn't quite woken up yet. If I needed to really wake them up, we would say the letters in reverse order. When it comes to our own happiness, everyone needs their own version of the alphabet exercise from time to time. We sometimes need to take energetic action – whether the energy is mental or physical – to help us on our happiness journey.

Beware of the kind of energy you surround yourself with and which you inject into your life, though. Have you ever been around people who always appear to be negative about their lives and seem to start each sentence with a sigh? Those people exude negative energy and, unlike with magnets, where opposite polarities attract, when it comes to emotional energy, like definitely attracts like. If you surround yourself with negative people, you start to view the world and the people in it with a negative slant.

In 'The Happiness Advantage' Shaun Achor talks about how focusing on negatives results in our brains perceiving reality as mostly negative. He references research[9] showing that law students suffer from dangerously elevated levels of stress. He mentions that law students told him that just being in the vicinity of other law students 'spread negative stress like second-hand smoke'.

There are occasions, however, when you can use negative energy and turn it into a positive. In her book, 'The Journey', Debra Searle describes the derogatory comments she endured from other rowers before entering the race, centring around her being a woman, and one of petite stature at that. She then goes on to explain how she stopped wasting emotional energy, putting the negative comments to good use instead:

"I took every negative comment and stored them all away in the back of my head. I used to think 'when I get out there in those 30 foot waves

9. Peterson, T.D., Peterson, E.W., (2009) 'Stemming the tide of law student depression: what law schools need to learn from the science of positive psychology', Yale Journal of Health Policy, Law and Ethics, 9, 357-434

I am going to think of you and what you just said to me and I'm going to burn it as fuel."

This doesn't mean, of course, that spreading negative energy is a goal we should all pursue in the hope that the recipients of such energy will turn it into fuel to propel them forward. Which kind of person would you rather be? The kind of person that lights up a room and puts a smile on people's faces, or one that drags everyone else around them down into their own misery? Put out your own positive energy in the world and you'll be rewarded, as much more positivity will come your way. Try smiling when you walk into a room and you will spread a ripple effect of positivity.

Over to you...
Try this when you walk into a shop:

Connect with the shop assistant by making eye contact and smiling. End with a 'thank you'.

How does it feel? Did they smile back? Did you feel a human connection?

Don't worry if they don't smile back. Not everybody is working on their happiness and positive energy as you are, but this shouldn't deter you from your personal journey. Try again the next time you're in a shop. More people will smile back than not.

Singing and dancing with abandon are also great tools to inject energy into your quest for fundamental happiness. Just about every culture in the world encompasses elements of music and dance. Young babies, as soon as they are able to sit unsupported, spontaneously dance along to music, even if their dance is merely an enthusiastic jiggling of their upper bodies. Every now and again, turn your favourite music up loud and sing and dance along as if nothing else matters in the world. At that moment, nothing else will matter. Immerse yourself in the joyfulness of that moment. The uplifting effects last beyond those initial euphoric few minutes.

Julie told me how she 'stops everything in its tracks' with her 'pink magic' and creating 'the wonder that is Kitchen Disco'.

She will sometimes initiate a spontaneous dance around the kitchen with music turned up very loud and where the entire family joins in. It's a tension release and a means of creating positive energy in the house when people are feeling down about something. It works. It lifts the mood and not just in the moment. The effects may not last forever, but they last for a while.

I have always enjoyed dance; from a very early age, I did ballet throughout my childhood and almost into my teens. I then moved onto modern dance and aerobics classes. I have taken salsa lessons, belly-dancing lessons and burlesque 'chair dancing' classes. As a teenager, our entire form at school took ballroom dancing lessons together once a week after school, culminating in an end of course ball. I even went to Zumba classes for a while, though after I tore a few fibres in one of my calf muscles, I decided that perhaps I needed some gentler exercise until I've lost more weight, to avoid further injury. Dancing combines, in my opinion, the best elements of positive physical energy - music and physical movement.

Positive energy can come from many sources; something as small as a smile can cause huge ripples. Positive energy has the power to spread, too. Look at how many motivational quotes and images are circulated virally around social networks on the internet.

Physical exercise is widely recommended by the medical profession as not only a healthy thing to do generally for our bodies, but a way to keep our minds healthy. It is often recommended as a means of keeping depression at bay or to help overcome depression for those already affected.

> *"No one in our society needs to be told that exercise is good for you. Whether you are overweight, or have a chronic illness or are a slim couch potato, you've probably heard or read this dictum countless times throughout your life. But has anyone told you, indeed, guaranteed you, that regular physical activity will make you happier? I swear by it."*
> *Sonja Lyubomirsky*

I am hardly the paragon of physical fitness. I definitely don't spend enough time on physical activity and exercise. I do, however, know that my personal experience backs up what medical professionals keep telling us and what Sonja Lyubomirsky swears by. When I undertake physical exercise, I feel better.

Physical exercise doesn't have to mean going to the gym for an hour every day. Little things make a difference. Whenever we go on holiday as a family, we end up doing a lot of walking as a natural part of the holiday, because we inevitably do some sight-seeing. Even as an over-forty, overweight woman who doesn't exercise much, I enjoy the walking parts of our holidays; they energise me, in more ways than one. Not only do I get the physical and mental benefit of the exercise itself, but I feel proud of myself for managing to walk for hours, or up a steep hill, or whatever that day's achievement is, deriving an additional positive emotional benefit from that sense of achievement. I am also convinced my legs look marvellous as a result of all the walking by the end of the holiday. Perhaps they really do look better, or maybe I just feel like they do.

A study[10] carried out by Dr Katherine Appleton of Queen's University Belfast, showed that we may perceive positive changes to body image after just two weeks of moderate exercise, despite there being no change to body weight or shape.

Charlie is undertaking the 'Duke of Edinburgh – Silver' programme at school. This means she will have to do quite a lot of walking to prepare for the three-day expedition that forms part of the requirement for the

10. Appleton, K. M., (2013), '6 x 40 mins exercise improves body image, even though body weight and shape do not change', Journal of Health Psychology, Vol 18 no 1, 110-120

award to be granted. As part of her work towards obtaining the award, she has also committed to an hour of physical activity per week for a set period of time. I am delighted that she chose to go swimming for an hour a week for a whole year. When she asked me to take her swimming every week, we decided it would be fun to do it as an activity together. This has been wonderful for both of us; we are both a lot fitter – this is noticeable in everyday activities – and we both feel great after each swimming session. As an added benefit, we get to spend that hour in the pool together – we swim a few laps but do lots of other exercises together; we race each other, run forwards, backwards and hop sideways or on one foot, to get from one point of the pool to another. Charlie cheats in all the races, incidentally, which causes us to have fits of laughter every time. We run around the 'flumes' area of our local swimming pool, carrying each other 'piggy-back' style in turns. What is there not to enjoy? How can this activity be anything but uplifting?

Over to you...
What physical exercise do you already do? How does it make you feel? (Tip: If you don't enjoy the physical exercise you do, keep trying different things until you find something you do enjoy. It shouldn't be a chore!)

What (additional) physical exercise could you incorporate into your life?

Make a list of the physical activities you can undertake and then take active steps to actually do them: if you need to find out about classes, research them, phone up and find out, then book yourself on. If you want to go for walks every weekend, plan your weekends in such a way that you have the time to do the walks. You could even just start by placing items out of your reach in your office so you need to leave your chair to get them.

Take action!

Your happiness (and overall well-being) is in your hands.

There are additional ways you can energise yourself and boost your happiness. Positive energy comes in many forms.

Tracie *says:*

"I like to take time to myself (usually not long in my crazy household) to just breathe.

Maybe look really closely at a flower, watch cars go by, watch my husband and boys when they think I'm not paying any attention; fishing… if at the coast, just watching the waves roll in. If I can't do these things I can close my eyes and picture them."

Laughter is also a great way to boost your happiness. So, what can you do to make yourself laugh more? It could be that you need to spend time with people you know are funny, or go to a comedy club, watch the DVD of your favourite comedian or even take yourself online and watch comedy clips on YouTube. Laughter has many health benefits and a huge one is to boost our emotional well-being. Laughter is a fantastic energiser. Make sure you include plenty of it in your life, especially when you are feeling low. In the next chapter 'S*!t Happens', we explore how seeing the humour – albeit, sometimes a dark humour – in horrifically traumatic situations, can make those situations more bearable and also make it less painful to remember them afterwards.

Another key way to energise yourself is to get enough sleep. It sounds simple enough, but most of us are guilty of neglecting this essential ingredient in our Recipe for Happiness when our lives get hectic and we cannot find enough hours in our days. A study[11] of subjects' reactions to facial expressions at different times of the day, with or without a daytime nap, showed that sleep, especially in the REM (Rapid Eye Movement) phase, contributes to enhanced ratings of positive (happy) expressions, whereas lack of sleep makes us more reactive to anger and fear.

Combine this with the fact that research[12] carried out on customer service representatives found that work performance was negatively affected if employees started the day in a negative mood; the relationship between sleep and happiness becomes even more apparent. If you are tired, you will be far more tuned in to negative emotions than positive ones and you won't work as well. I know that when I over-do it and

11. Gujar, N., McDonald, S., Nishida, M., and Walker, M. (2010). 'A Role for REM Sleep in Recalibrating the Sensitivity of the Human Brain to Specific Emotions', Cerebral Cortex, 21 (1), 115-123

12. Wilk, S., Ohio State University, (April 2011) 'Got up on the wrong side of the bed? Your work will show it', Public Release

work long hours, I end up feeling tearful and over-react to the slightest negative event in my day. At times in my life when I have over-stretched myself, although it may have seemed counter-intuitive to work less, I found this to be the best way to get myself back on track: to simply stop, take some time out and get some sleep can work wonders.

What do you do to energise yourself?

The phrase 'make some 'me' time' may sound a little new-age, but that doesn't make it any less essential. Sometimes, in our increasingly hectic lives, we need to stop and take stock. Maybe a hot bath at the end of a long day is how you relax and release negative or nervous energy you've stored up in your body and mind all day. Maybe it is something more physical such as dancing or exercise. Everybody 'ticks' differently - you need to examine your life and look at when you are at your lowest and highest points, and what triggers one or the other state. Find the triggers for your positivity. Add them to your life as little happiness ingredients.

> *"In a virtuous circle, research shows, being happy energizes you, and at the same time, having more energy makes it easier for you to engage in activities – like socializing and exercise – that boost happiness."*
> Gretchen Rubin

Pizza

Pizza

Making pizza requires energy. A lot of physical energy goes into making the dough and then rolling it out into a pizza shape (you'll notice on the photo above that rounded perfection is not required). A very hot oven is required to achieve the perfect pizza, albeit for a very short time; ideally, a pizza needs to be cooked in a wood-fired, stone pizza oven, but failing that, a very hot home oven will work. When I took the photo shown above, I used a pizza stone in a gas-fired lidded barbecue for five minutes. It worked perfectly!

Making pizza is easier than many people think. Here is a simple recipe to make the dough and cook it with toppings of your choice.

Ingredients for the pizza dough (this will make approx. 6 thin pizzas)
- 500ml water
- 1tsp white sugar
- 2tbsp dried yeast
- 1kg plain white flour, plus flour for sprinkling
- 8tbsp extra virgin olive oil
- 4tsp sea salt

Ingredients for the pizza topping
- Tomato passata or 'sugo al pomodoro' (basic tomato sauce, see http://bit.ly/sugo_pomodoro)
- Optional: Oregano (if not already included in 'sugo al pomodoro')

- Extra virgin olive oil
- Mozzarella, torn into tiny pieces by hand
- Any other toppings you would like to add, e.g. ham, etc

Method

Mix the sugar in a bowl with 200ml hand-hot water.

Sprinkle in the dried yeast and whisk, then leave to stand for 10-15 mins until the watery yeast mixture has formed a thick froth.

Dissolve the sea salt in approximately 100ml of warm water.

Meanwhile, place the flour into a large bowl and make a well in the middle.

When the yeast, water and sugar mixture is ready, pour this into the well in the middle of the flour. Add the water and salt solution plus the olive oil and approximately 200ml of warm water. Don't add all the water at once, as the exact quantities will vary depending on how much water the flour absorbs. Mix by hand until it begins to form a dough, then pour this onto a kitchen work surface.

Knead vigorously until you have a smooth, pliable and elastic dough. Roll this into a ball.

Sprinkle some flour into the now-empty bowl that you used to start making the dough and place the dough ball back into the bowl. Take a clean tea-towel and run it under hot water, then wring it out to ensure it doesn't drip. Place it over the bowl containing the dough. Leave the dough to rise in a warm and dry place for 1.5 - 2 hours.

Once the dough is ready, it will have roughly doubled in size.

Preheat the oven to the highest setting (or use a lidded BBQ on a high setting) and preheat a pizza stone in the oven/BBQ.

Tear a piece of dough (the size of a large fist) and shape it into a thick round(ish) shape by hand, then place it onto a lightly floured surface; using a rolling pin, roll it out until it is very thin (almost transparent if you want a really thin pizza), rotating it so that you can use the rolling pin to create an even thickness.

Remove the preheated pizza stone from the oven; place the thin sheet of pizza dough onto it. Then, very quickly, add the other ingredients:

Spread on a thin layer of tomato passata or 'sugo al pomodoro', sprinkle with oregano (optional) and a light drizzle of extra virgin olive oil. Add any other ingredients you wish to add, e.g. thin strips of ham.

Sprinkle on the torn pieces of mozzarella (lightly - you are not aiming for a full, heavy covering of cheese).
If adding black olives, place these on top of the cheese at the end.

Place the pizza stone with the topped pizza back into the oven or BBQ, close the door/lid and cook for approximately 5 minutes (possibly a bit longer in the oven) until the pizza crust is crisp with a few brown parts and the cheese is bubbling, with a slight golden crust beginning to form in parts.

Remove from the oven/BBQ and serve immediately.

Repeat the process with the other pizzas.

This is great fun for parties - children love to join in and add the toppings, but be careful of the hot pizza stone!

Note: You can also use the dough to make focaccia.

Ingredients:
- Pizza dough
- Rosemary (fresh or dried)
- Coarse sea salt
- Extra virgin olive oil

Method:
Make the dough as for the pizza recipe.
Preheat the oven to 250°C.

Spread a generous amount of extra virgin olive oil onto an oven tray.

Roll out the dough to a 1cm thick square/rectangle

and place onto the oiled tray.

Using your fingertips, make some indentations in the surface of the dough. Sprinkle on some coarse sea salt and rosemary and drizzle on some extra-virgin olive oil.

Place in the oven for approximately 10 minutes, until the dough is cooked and the surface has begun to turn golden.

Serve hot or cold on its own, or sliced open and filled with mozzarella and ham, like a sandwich.

S*!t Happens!

"No life – if we live long enough – is without stress, adversity or crisis. The possibilities are endless – the death of a loved one, a grave illness, an accident, victimization, a natural disaster, a terrorist attack, domestic violence, poverty, stigmatization, divorce and job loss."
Sonja Lyubomirsky

Bad things happen to everyone in life. The scale may be different; the perception of gravity of an event may differ – what may have a major impact on one person could be perceived as a minor inconvenience by another. Ultimately, though, as Sonja Lyubomirsky states, we are all subject at some point or another in our lives to events that cause us physical or emotional pain.

It is therefore up to us to decide how we handle these events and how we let ourselves be affected by them. Most of us probably know at least one person who appears to have a very good life yet does nothing but complain about how nothing ever goes their way, day in, day out. What makes those people different to those that appear to take things in their stride? Why do the easy-going people also appear to have better luck than those that always complain and have a negative attitude towards everything that happens in their lives?

In 'Citipaper' on 21st March 1996, Annette Earling explained 'The Tetris Effect', a term she found in an online Journal, 'Risks Digest', in an article by Garth Kidd. Garth wrote: "There's a local nickname for the long-term effects of immersion games or simulations – it's the 'Tetris Effect'." Annette explained in her article how she had found herself experiencing 'The Tetris Effect' after discovering the 'Tetris' computer game and playing it for many hours on end, as it is so addictive. She suddenly found herself seeing the 'Tetris' blocks everywhere. "Walking through the aisles at the local Acme, trying to decide between Honey Nut or the new Frosted Cheerios, I notice how perfectly one set of cereal boxes would fit in with the gap on the row below it. Running doggedly around the track at the Y, bored out of my mind, I find myself focusing on the brick wall and calculating which direction I'd have to rotate those slightly darker bricks to make them fit in with the uneven row of dark bricks a few feet lower down the wall. Going out to get some fresh air after hours of work, I rub my watery, stinging eyes, look up at the Philadelphia skyline , and wonder, 'If I flip the Victory Building on its side, would it fit into the gap between Liberties One and Two?'."

I can certainly identify with how Annette feels as I have experienced 'The Tetris Effect' myself. When I was at university, before the advent of the internet, a favoured procrastination tool amongst students was playing 'Minesweeper' on the computer. I played this so much that I used to see those little squares and exploding mines everywhere, even in my dreams. In similar fashion, when I worked in one company where the 'phones were ringing incessantly, constantly interrupting our workflow, I used to 'hear' the same 'phones ringing at home in the evenings and at weekends. My brain was so used to hearing that annoying ring every few minutes, that I imagined it when it wasn't there. In the mid-90s, I used to watch a TV series called 'My So-Called Life', in which actress Clare Danes played a typical teenager going through her daily life, suffering from a certain amount of 'Teenage Angst'. Even though I was in my twenties, I found myself emulating her emotions and mannerisms and started feeling mildly depressed and, well, 'Teenage Angst'-ridden after every episode.

What does 'The Tetris Effect' have to do with persistently negative people?

In 'The Happiness Advantage', Shaun Achor likens this to the psychological term of 'cognitive afterimage' and relates this to people being "unable to break a pattern of thinking or behaving". Sometimes this pattern can be negative. He goes on to say that "These people aren't trying to be difficult or grumpy. Their brains are just really outstanding at scanning their environment for negatives". He then goes on to say that we can retrain our brains to "scan for the good things in life".

When I first joined one recruitment company, I had a really difficult time. I worked with colleagues that had difficulty in accepting me as part of the team and, for whatever reason, it took me a long time – six months, I think – before I eventually made my first placement. During this time, one of the colleagues that didn't like me very much asked me in a sardonic tone, 'Are you worried at all?'

'About what?' I answered.

'The fact you haven't made any placements yet,' was her reply.

I smiled and my response was, 'No, because I know it will happen.' There was, perhaps, more bravado in my statement than actual conviction, but I do believe that I had trained my brain to scan for the good things and therefore expected things to turn out well. As it happens, she left the company shortly afterwards, whereas I did go on to make my first, and many subsequent placements prior to eventually becoming a Director and shareholder in the business.

On the subject of perceptions and attitudes, Matthieu Ricard goes further by examining the relationship between suffering and happiness:

"Suffering can be triggered by numerous causes over which we sometimes have some power, and sometimes none. […] Unhappiness is altogether different, being the way in which we experience our suffering."

It is possible, therefore, to experience painful or traumatic events in our lives, or go through periods of extreme stress, without actually being unhappy. This comes back to the concept of fundamental happiness mentioned previously in this book.

Once you realise that your suffering does not mean you are fundamentally unhappy, you also realise that it is temporary and that you will therefore be able to return to your fundamentally happy state once the situation you are in is resolved or you are ready to move on and put it behind you.

Furthermore, once you realise that "S*!t Happens" to everyone, that the universe hasn't singled you out for extra doses of bad luck, you will find it easier to look for learning opportunities in painful life events. Perhaps you'll even see the humour in certain situations.

There have been a number of occasions in my life where a sense of humour has got me through painful circumstances. There is a reason why there are terms such as 'gallows humour'[13]. At times of extreme emotional stress, we need to relieve the tension, a bit like letting steam out of a pressure cooker through the release valve to avoid an explosion.

When Hannah was in intensive care after her open heart surgery, she was a very angry baby every time she was awake, thrashing about all over the place. It's understandable; she was probably in considerable discomfort and some amount of pain a lot of the time. When babies have cannulae inserted into their arms or legs, they often have foam supports strapped to them to avoid excessive bending of their arms and help keep the cannulae in place. Hannah had both her arms strapped up in this way, as she had a lot of tubes going in and out of her body all over the place. This meant that both her arms were essentially rigid and unable to bend at the elbow. As she thrashed about

13. Gallows humour (noun): grim and ironical humour in a desperate or hopeless situation (Source: http://www.oxforddictionaries.com)

in a semi-conscious state and lashed out, this turned her arms into something akin to weapons, ready to be wielded at any approaching doctor or nurse. Hannah was still in grave danger and taking a long time to recover from her surgery, suffering from various complications along the way. Her 'karate-chopping' movements aimed at doctors and nurses were a big source of amusement to us all and the laughter helped us through that difficult time. We still joke about it with her now and Hannah loves to hear the stories of her times in hospital.

Sometimes, when "S*!t Happens", it also serves a purpose: it allows us to learn something. In my student days, at the end of the summer holiday leading into my second year at Bradford University, I had a rather disconcerting experience.

The night before my car journey from Luxembourg to Bradford, which was to include an overnight ferry from Rotterdam to Hull, I began experiencing some strange sensations in my mouth that caused me to repeatedly draw in saliva in an exaggerated manner, but I didn't pay much attention to this. I set off in the car the following day and as my journey on the motorway progressed, my body started doing strange things. My head started turning involuntarily to one side and would remain there before suddenly snapping back to the front. It felt akin to something out of the film "The Exorcist". I was terrified. Of course, I should have stopped the car and called for help – though this was before the days of mobile 'phones – but I was young and frightened and wasn't thinking straight. I even managed to convince myself that something had happened to my brain and I would stay like this forever. All rational thought had deserted me.

Somehow, driving very cautiously and slowly, I made it to the ferry terminal in Rotterdam. Once there, I had to wait a few hours before driving the car onto the ferry, during which time my symptoms worsened. My head movements became more violent and it was turning so far it was hurting my neck. My drawing in of saliva was constant and compulsive. My legs started shaking uncontrollably.

Once I got onto the ferry, I somehow made it to my cabin, where I attempted to lie down on my berth. I soon realised that I absolutely needed help. As I lay on my back, my involuntary head movements were so strong that my back would arch and lift off the berth. This really was turning into a horror movie where I had the starring role! I took myself to the reception desk and asked: 'Is there a doctor on board?'. Luckily, they had a medical officer. I described my symptoms – though they didn't need much description as they were pretty obvious – and he asked, 'Have you been taking any medication?'

I replied that I'd become ill with gastroenteritis a couple of days previously and that, in light of my imminent travel, my family doctor had prescribed Metoclopramide to stop me from vomiting. The medical officer looked it up and it transpired that involuntary movements are just some of the rare but possible side effects that Metoclopramide can cause to the central nervous system.

He advised me to stop taking the tablets immediately and called the poisons unit in Amsterdam for advice. Following this, he gave me some charcoal tablets to line my stomach, followed by a hefty dose of Valium to counter the effects of the Metoclopramide. He put me in a very plush and spacious cabin near his office with instructions to pull the emergency cord if necessary, leaving me to sleep it off. Eventually, my body calmed down enough for me to get a couple of hours' sleep before arriving in Hull the next morning. No further exorcism was required and I was back to normal.

This was a useful experience for me, not only because of the immense comedy value when I told the story to my friends when back in Bradford, but because I learnt to always read the patient leaflet that comes with any medication. Of course, if we took every possible side effect of medications on board, we'd never take any tablets at all. Painkillers you take for headaches 'may cause headaches'; medication to settle your stomach or intestines 'may cause nausea, vomiting or diarrhoea' and the list goes on. I do know, however, that if I had read the patient leaflet before taking Metoclopramide, I would have stopped taking the tablets as soon as I started experiencing those very disturbing side effects, because I would have realised they were caused by the medication.

There are times when "S*!t Happens" and it forces us to reassess our current circumstances and make decisions. Having worked so hard to keep one of my businesses going over the past few years, I often got frustrated and scared; I had no income and our family savings were dwindling. I realised that I couldn't simply keep doing what I'd always done - I needed to change something so that I could change the outcome. The opportunity came to help another business with their social media marketing activities, and 'Social Media Marketing Angel' was born.

I also applied to take part in a TV show that was aimed at taking food from a home kitchen, or very early commercial stages, to a point where it could be marketed on a larger scale. As Supplì/Arancini (see recipe at the end of this chapter) were not widely available in the U.K. and hardly anyone had heard of them, I saw a gap in the market and was encouraged by the fact that these little balls of deliciousness had started appearing in gastro pubs and in London food markets. These places often mark the emergence of new food trends that will spread U.K.-wide in time. I was accepted onto the programme, enlisted the help of my friend and business partner, Lisa, and after we'd completed a few mad days of filming, I thought, 'I can do this. I'll set it up as a business!'

For the best part of a year, while trying to juggle far too many balls (pardon the pun), I created recipes, put food safety processes in place and bought equipment; I achieved a five-star hygiene rating for my home kitchen, sold the products at markets, got a buzz going on social media platforms, built a website, obtained testimonials and even got the products into a few retailers. In some ways, the business was a huge success. I couldn't keep the momentum going, however, and knew the only way I could keep going and actually earn, rather than lose, money in this venture, was to scale up to a small production facility so that I could focus on sales and marketing while others made and packaged the product. This would also give me the opportunity to produce and sell more, though I'd need some kind of distribution system in place. All of this required funds I didn't have, and for me to obtain those funds, if that had been at all possible, would have meant putting everything on the line and putting my house at risk. At that point, I didn't feel the risk was worth taking. Maybe the timing was wrong; there were too many things going on in my life and I was under a great deal of stress. Maybe the figures just wouldn't have stacked up, no matter when or how I did it. I made the difficult decision to walk away. It was the right decision to make, even though it was painful at the time. It freed up a lot of time for me, allowing me to focus on other things, including writing this book. Walking away also gave my family our home and kitchen back. Walking away meant that I can now finally enjoy eating risotto again and I once again love eating Supplì.

The last few years have been challenging and I probably have less money or financial stability now than I have ever had, but I am in a much better place. I have businesses that are growing and a steady stream of work that's keeping the proverbial wolf from the door. I love my work and enjoy the daily challenges it brings. I can manage my time in such a way that I can take a few days off to spend with life-long friends I don't see very often. I can go to school plays and concerts. My mind is more open than ever to all the opportunities before me and I firmly believe that things will work out absolutely fine because I'm doing everything I can to make that happen. Had the economic crisis not forced my hand by a series of events that led to me investing in the business that employed me, I may never have taken the entrepreneurial plunge to start my own business in the first place.

Kath went through some traumatic experiences but she can now see that her particular "S*!t Happens" events have resulted in positive *outcomes.*

She told me:
"S*!t happens; it's how you deal with it that counts. Years ago I had a stillbirth, which was truly awful. And then I lost my next baby at 24 weeks and had to have an operation to remove it. It took me a long time to get anything positive from those experiences, but later on in life I realised that I would not have been able to give my only child, Nicola, all the music lessons and purchase all the musical instruments, etc if I had had three children – my funds would not have stretched to that. Nicola went on to get a first class honours degree (majoring in music and drama) and, later on, another teaching degree. She has now blessed me with two gorgeous grandkids who I adore!"

It may take a long time before we can use the benefit of hindsight to find the positives in traumatic events that happen in our lives, but if we give it time and then look hard enough, we can usually find something positive emerging from the ashes of our previous pain.

Over to you...
Think back to a previous stressful event or crisis in your life; make a list of any positive outcomes that have eventually resulted from it.

Go one step further and try to find some funny anecdotes from that time in your life, if you can. These will help you remember the events in a less painful way and allow you to focus on where you are now and how your past situation may have helped you get here, even though it may have felt desperate at the time.

Suppli

Suppli
Breaded Risotto Balls

Suppli - short for "Suppli al telefono" - is the name used in Rome/the Lazio Region. In Sicily and other parts of Southern Italy they are known as "Arancini".

They are little round or egg-shaped risotto shapes, breaded and deep fried, sometimes containing a nugget of mozzarella at the centre, and they can be made with any type of risotto base.

The Roman/Lazio "Suppli al Telefono" (called that way because, when cut in half, the two halves are on a 'telephone wire' to each other via the stringy melted cheese) tend to be more oval-shaped, whereas "Arancini" can have round, oval or tear-drop shapes. I tend to make them all into small, round morsels as they are easier to shape and easier to eat as a snack or appetiser. They make fabulous party food!

Suppli are usually served in traditional "Pizzerie" (Pizza Restaurants) as 'antipasti' (starters).

These delicious morsels occupy a special place in my heart and in this book. In my heart, because I have so often enjoyed them in Rome with family and they bring back happy memories; in this book and specifically this chapter, because when my mind opened itself up to new opportunities, I also took a giant leap of faith with regard to this delicious food.

Suppli are not hugely difficult to make, though they

do require patience as they take time. It may take a few attempts before you get them right, but it's worth persevering. If you really don't want to make them yourself, do make sure you try them if you go to Rome. Or ask for Arancini in other parts of southern Italy, especially Naples and Sicily.

The recipe below is for small, round vegetarian ones (traditional Roman ones are larger and oval, and are made with a minced meat and tomato risotto base – similar to a bolognese sauce in a risotto – rather than a simple tomato and onion risotto base).

This recipe makes approximately 35-40 small (roughly golf ball sized) Suppli:

Ingredients:
- Tomato risotto made with 300g dry rice (see recipe – http://bit.ly/tomato_risotto – or buy a pre-prepared risotto)

  TIP: If you were making ordinary risotto, you would leave it quite 'wet', but for the suppli you need to ensure you don't have excess liquid. Also, bear in mind that the rice will become drier as it cools down and absorbs the last of the moisture.

- 75g soft fresh mozzarella (drained weight)
- 300-400g cheap, semi-stale, white bread made into breadcrumbs in a food blender

  TIP: place the breadcrumbs onto a large, deep

food-serving/oven tray. You won't use all the breadcrumbs but you'll need an ample supply of them in order to thoroughly coat the individual suppli

- 2 large eggs, lightly beaten
- 200g plain white flour – as with the breadcrumbs, you won't use all of it but you need plenty to roll the suppli in....put it in a large tray so you have ample space
- vegetable oil for frying

Method
- Leave the risotto to cool for a couple of hours or, ideally, in a fridge overnight
- Add vegetable oil to a medium saucepan until half full (approx. 3-4cm in depth) and place on the hob, on a medium-high heat, taking care never to let it over-heat and become smoky – or, heat oil in a deep fat fryer to 180°C
- Prepare yourself a little production line: the risotto, a bowl/plate containing the mozzarella (torn into small pieces), another bowl containing the plain white flour, one with the lightly beaten eggs and another containing the breadcrumbs

TIP: I like to use latex/vinyl gloves when rolling the suppli – it stops my hands from turning orange and also allows the fat from the risotto to stay on the rice rather than absorb into my hands, which makes it easier to coat the rice balls in flour. I also like to have a bowl of lukewarm water and a towel handy so that I can wash excess breadcrumbs from my hands between batches.

- Take a small handful of rice and squeeze it in the palm of your hand until it starts sticking together; roll it into a ball then, using your finger, poke a hole into the middle
- Place a piece of mozzarella into the hole, then close it up again and form a neat ball between the palms of your hands, ensuring that no mozzarella sticks out
- Lightly roll the rice ball in flour
- Dip the rice ball into the eggs
- Place the rice ball onto the breadcrumbs, then gather a good amount in your hands and cover the rice ball. Pick the rice ball up and compact the breadcrumbs further with the palms of your hands, ensuring an even (but not too thick) coating and so that there are no parts of the rice ball that have no coating

TIP: You can either repeat this process until all your rice balls are ready to fry or you can do them in batches of 3-4 and roll the next batch while you're frying the previous one; the latter method is faster, but if you're nervous about timings/burning the suppli, do the two steps separately.

- If using a pan rather than a deep-fat fryer, check the temperature of the oil: if you drop a few breadcrumbs into it the oil should 'fizz' but the breadcrumbs should slowly turn golden, not instantly brown/blacken (if that's the case, it's too hot – take it off the heat for a couple of minutes, then test again)

- Drop a batch of suppli (not too many – 3-4, depending on the size of the pan/fryer you're using) into the oil. You need to have enough oil in the pan for this to be a deep-frying process, so the suppli are fully immersed in hot oil without touching the bottom of the pan
- After 3-4 minutes, the suppli should be golden. Lift them out with a slotted spoon (or fryer basket) and rest them on a tray or plate, lined with absorbent paper (e.g. kitchen roll)
- Repeat the process until they are all cooked
- Serve after they have had a couple of minutes to cool down

TIP: You can make these a day in advance and then reheat them in the oven, at 180°C (fan-assisted, otherwise 200°C) for approx. 20 mins

Savour...

"If you're in the room, be in the room."
Nigel Risner

"When you 'stop and smell the roses' instead of walking by obliviously, you are savouring. When you bask and take pride in your own or your friends' accomplishments, you are savouring. When you suddenly emerge out of a frazzled or distracted state and become fully aware of how much there is to enjoy of life, you are savouring."
Sonja Lyubomirsky

Italians have a way of eating that transcends mere nourishment. An Italian family meal takes time. Enjoying the food, talking about the food, chatting to family members: these all become intertwined and it is the entire meal that is savoured in this way. Italian weddings feature multi-course feasts that last for hours, with plenty of time between each course to enjoy the company of the bride and groom and other guests.

I remember many happy summers at my mum's holiday home in the Italian Alps, in the Valle d'Aosta region, when we would hear the call come up the mountain from the neighbours' house below: 'Katja! Vieni a fare merenda? Venite giù!' ('Katja' – that's my mum – 'Will you come for a snack? Come down, all of you!'). Those were never 'snacks', they were feasts! There was a lot of traditional Italian savouring going on. We would spend the afternoon sitting in our neighbours' garden, eating various salamis, hams and cheeses with delicious rustic bread, usually accompanied by some great wine, until the afternoon became evening. At that point, someone would suggest that we might as well stay for dinner and they'd rustle up 'something quick'. After more eating and drinking, we'd make it home in the early hours of the morning. Of course, as the inhabitants of three or four friendly neighbouring houses would partake in these 'snacking' afternoons and evenings, another neighbour would reciprocate the invitation a couple of days later, then my mum would host everyone at our house, and so on. Dieting was definitely not on the cards during those summers!

In 'Eat, Pray, Love' Elizabeth Gilbert describes an ordinary October day in Rome that she will always count as one of the happiest of her life. She describes finding a market she hadn't previously spotted and buying some asparagus – while comfortably conversing with the stall-holder and her son in Italian – then returning home to truly savour a simple lunch of soft-boiled eggs, the asparagus she had just bought, some olives and a few pieces of goats' cheese, along with some salmon, followed by a juicy peach gifted to her by the stall-holder at the market. She describes being so awe-struck by the beauty of the food before her that she couldn't eat it for ages. Eventually she did eat – and savour – her meal. Her description of her feelings at the time is beautiful:
"Happiness inhabited my every molecule"

I believe life should be a little bit like Italian meals. We need to slow down the pace sometimes and stop to savour the little moments. In those little moments, we will find a myriad of little happiness ingredients we may otherwise overlook entirely. Whilst those moments may be fleeting and, in themselves, do not constitute happiness, they are essential to a happy life. Missing out on all the small constituents that add to life's greatness means we risk missing out on life – and the enjoyment thereof – altogether.

The 'Georgia Psychological Association' website features an article called 'Savoring the Moment' by Daniel H Johnston, Ph.D.
In this article, he writes: "Savoring the moment is simple in concept. It means to fully appreciate whatever we're experiencing. The problem is that in order to savor something we must be aware of it when it's happening, and with the frantic pace of modern life, many enjoyable moments pass us by because we often are distracted from or inattentive to them."

Here is what some of my interviewees told me about how they savour the little moments in life:

Marc *makes the most of his time with his wife and children. As a club DJ, he works at night, whilst his wife works during the day. This is great from a practical point of view as he's around to take the children to school, pick them up and so on, but doesn't do much for spending time together as a family. They therefore make the most of the time they do get to spend together and that doesn't necessarily mean making grand gestures or* plans; often they find the best moments to savour together are when they snuggle up on the sofa and watch TV together, or go to the cinema. The little things make all the difference.

Ashley W told me he loves to cook and loves to walk. He is happiest when he is in the kitchen with his pots and pans, totally immersed in creating a plate of food that gives pleasure to others. The same is true for him when walking out on the fells. This is where he is completely at ease with who he is.

Tracie put it very succinctly: 'My children and husband are springs of little spots of happiness.'

Ashley F Ashley tries to spend as much time as possible with her husband; they both enjoy travelling. She enjoys planning for the next holiday and has built her business up to 'feed the travelling habit' and help her husband leave his job so they can spend more time together. They both like the simple things: growing their own vegetables and herbs, for example. They both derive lots of pleasure from gardening and listening to the birds.

Cheryl has a passion for storms, which really requires her to truly seize and savour the moment: "I've loved thunderstorms for as long as I can remember. When I was a child, my Dad encouraged all his daughters to drop everything whenever there was a storm, and watch from our south-facing bedroom window. I spent time reading as much as I could about weather and storms and he was really encouraging.

This has led to a lifelong passion. Storms are beautiful but fleeting, and you have to seize the moment and get out there if you want to see them properly. I love going storm chasing and I've seen some fantastic sights over the years - vivid forked lightning, spectacular night-time storms, mammatus, funnel clouds, even ball lightning. I was once thrown across a room by a nearby lightning bolt which was probably my scariest moment!"

I'm a Skywarn U.K. Spotter and part of that role involves reporting severe weather, which we do get in the U.K., though not on the same scale as the U.S. I can't imagine not being interested in storms - it's a huge part of who I am. Luckily, I have a very understanding husband who also loves storms, and my sisters and friends always keep me informed about what's brewing in their neck of the woods!"

Fran and Derek *make a lovely couple. Fran keeps a 'memories drawer' with ticket stubs from concerts and other events they have gone to together, special photographs that remind her of days they have spent and enjoyed together and lots of other little mementoes. Even now they share a home, Fran still gathers little reminders of the wonderful times they spend together and last Christmas, she gave Derek a delightful present. She made him a 'memories book', which they both kindly allowed me to take a few snapshots of and share with the readers of this book:*

This is what Daniel H Johnston, Ph.D., would call the 'memory building' technique for savouring the moment: 'You engage in memory building by capturing a mental image of the moment or by taking a souvenir'.

I try to savour as many of the little things in life as I can. For example, both my daughters used to come into my bed in the mornings for a cuddle before they got up properly to get ready for school. Eventually, Charlie grew out of this. Hannah still does this most mornings and gets quite annoyed with me if I need to be up earlier for a meeting and we miss out on our morning cuddle. I am delighted that she still wants to spend this special time with me now she is fourteen and I really savour those few minutes every day. Despite her constant insistence that she will keep doing this forever I am very aware that she will eventually outgrow this stage, so I need to make the most of it while it lasts.

I also love spending time in the kitchen, cooking

special meals, recreating my grandmother's recipes or experimenting with ingredients to create new ones. I am completely in my element at those times and try to get as many opportunities to do this as possible. At times, I catch myself standing in the kitchen with a huge silly grin on my face while I'm cooking! Whilst I don't enjoy mundane day-to-day cooking quite as much, I love it when Simon and I cook together, splitting tasks up between us and exchanging playful banter while we do this. With busy lives pulling us in all directions, this can sometimes be the only meaningful time we get to spend together, so we make the most of it. It's often at these times that one of us will spontaneously exclaim to the other 'I love you, you know!' and, should we dare to have a cheeky kiss while we're at it, we're bound to be interrupted by one of our daughters telling us to 'stop being so gross and get a room'. Happy times!

There are other tiny events in life that are so easy to miss if we don't make the time to stop and savour them. My life is hectic, so I don't always make the time to stop and take notice, but I do make a conscious effort to do it more and more frequently, because I know it makes me feel good and contributes to my fundamental happiness. We have a buddleia bush outside the bay window of our living room; it has a tendency to overhang our drive at the front of the house when it grows huge in summer. Buddleias are also known as the 'butterfly bush' for their butterfly-attracting properties. We have had this plant for years, but somehow I had never paid much attention to the butterflies (though I did appreciate the prettiness of the plant itself, which Simon had specifically planted because he knew I liked the colours). This year, I was suddenly struck by the beauty and quantity of the two species of butterfly that spent so much time on the flowers. Every time I drove anywhere, I would be mesmerised when I pulled the car onto the drive. It costs nothing to stop for a minute and just admire beauty. Every time I did this, I would feel a deep sense of contentment that would last well beyond the moment. On one occasion, I went outside especially on a sunny morning to take some photos of the butterflies. I posted them on Facebook to share the beauty and lots of people joined the online conversation. This would come under the savouring technique of 'sharing' that Daniel H Johnston Ph.D. refers to.

When 'memory building' or 'sharing' as part of the savouring process, do find the right balance, however, as you may end up missing out on the 'savouring' part altogether if you are too wrapped up in keeping a record of all events worth savouring. We live in an age where so many people share everything on Facebook and Twitter as soon as it happens, sometimes detrimentally towards enjoyment of the event itself. Even before the advent of social networking, there was a risk of 'memory building' taking over. I remember my aunt taking lots of photos of all family gatherings throughout my childhood. She was rarely seen without a camera in her hand. When she had her own children, she filmed and photographed every school play, every concert and every party. Eventually, she realised she was so busy creating memories for the future that she wasn't enjoying the present, so she drastically cut down on her photographic endeavours.

Each season brings with it other beautiful moments we can savour. The melancholy of a foggy, rainy autumn day with the stunning colours of leaves everywhere; the crispness of a winter's day with blue skies above and white snow on the ground. The hopefulness of spring with its cheeky rain showers and tentatively warm and sunny days, accompanied by new life everywhere: lambs in fields, new flowers blooming, trees regaining their lost foliage. Beauty is all around us if we just stop to notice it and truly take it in and savour it. Once you get into the habit of paying more attention, you notice more and more awe-inspiring moments of greatness all around you.

It is when savouring these moments that you can build up a store of happiness, a bit like recharging a battery. If your stores are high enough, when you do find yourself in happiness-draining situations, you will hopefully not completely deplete your happiness stores; a little bit of fundamental happiness will remain and this will give you the strength to overcome adversity and start building up the happiness levels again in future.

In NLP, there is a practice known as 'anchoring'. This is a method whereby you can store and later trigger at will 'states', such as feeling contented, a sense of success or achievement, etc. This is done by a combination of strong visualisation techniques, combined with setting a 'trigger point' on your body, such as pinching your earlobe or squeezing thumb and forefinger together, for example. Once you have set those trigger points and anchored your desired state, you can trigger it any time you want. This technique can be very useful to boost your happiness level at times when you are feeling low, or to boost your confidence before a stressful or scary event, such as a job interview or sales presentation. David Molden and Pat Hutchinson describe the anchoring technique very clearly and simply in their book, 'Brilliant NLP' (pp. 31-33).

Over to you...
Take a few quiet moments to contemplate your day so far.

What did you see, hear, do, smell, taste, and touch? What moments did you savour? Spend a few minutes to write these down and recall how you felt at the time. Savour them all over again. Reminisce.

Make a conscious effort to pay more attention to the little moments worth savouring in life from now on.

Whatever your little happiness ingredients are, whatever it is that makes you stop what you're doing and gaze or listen in awe, make sure you savour the little moments in life. And when you can, without over-doing it, find a way to store those emotions to relive in the future, whether it's via anchoring the state you're in, keeping a memories drawer or book, or sharing great moments via Facebook/a traditional photo album.

> *"Life moves pretty fast...if you don't stop and look around every once in a while, you could miss it!"*
> *Ferris Bueller (character in 'Ferris Bueller's Day Off' Motion Picture, Paramount, 1986)*

Tiramisù

Tiramisù
(Literally translated as 'pick me up')

I simply had to end this chapter - and the book - on this particular recipe. Not only is it what my friends and family ask for the most and which therefore qualifies as my 'signature dish', but it is the ultimate indulgent, rich dessert that demands you savour every mouthful. Let's face it, if you're going to eat that many calories in one go, you may as well savour and enjoy every single one of them and make them count!

What most people don't realise is that tiramisù is incredibly quick and simple to make. It is essentially a dish of pure assembly and requires no cooking whatsoever. You can make it in about 20 minutes, then leave it in the fridge overnight to delight your tastebuds the following day.

Ingredients
(for approximately 8 people - you will need a very large dish to make this in):
- 2-3 packets sponge finger biscuits
- 500g mascarpone
- 6 large fresh eggs
- 200g caster sugar
- A good slosh of 'Marsala all'Uovo' liqueur (if you can't get any, it works well with rum or Tia Maria, but the authentic taste only comes from using the correct drink...Marsala would work, too, but it hasn't had the eggs and sugar added to

give it the distinctive 'Marsala all'Uovo' taste)
- A bowl of cold black coffee (use espresso, ideally), mixed with another generous glug of 'Marsala all'Uovo'
- Cocoa powder
- Pinch of salt

Method:

Whisk the egg yolks and sugar in a very large bowl until light in colour and fluffy in texture. Add some 'Marsala all'Uovo' (to taste) and whisk again.

Add the mascarpone and whisk the mixture until smooth - check for taste and add more 'Marsala all'Uovo' if required.

Add a pinch of salt to the egg whites and whisk them until stiff (you should be able to turn the bowl upside down without the fluffy whites moving).

Gently fold the stiff egg whites into the egg yolk and mascarpone mixture.

Dip enough biscuits, one at a time (brief dip only - don't let them go soggy) into the coffee and 'Marsala all'Uovo' mixture to form a bottom layer in the dish. Cover with some of the mascarpone mixture.

Repeat until the dish is full, finishing with the mascarpone mixture (ensure you save enough for this final, rich layer and remember, the deeper the dish, the better the Tiramisù...try to have as many layers as you can).

TIP: Alternate the direction you lay the biscuits for each layer, so they're criss-crossing each other from one layer to the next.

Finish it all off by sprinkling some cocoa powder over the top.

Refrigerate — it's best served the following day.

Acknowledgements

So many people have contributed to this book, whether they realise it or not. It would be impossible to list everyone, as every person that has somehow touched my life has, in some way, contributed to this book.

I would like to thank Gail Powell and Diane Hall of Solopreneur Publishing for their belief in me, their guidance and their patience with my numerous revisions; letting go is possibly one of the hardest parts when writing a book!

All the people I have encountered not only in my personal life but in my business life have had an influence on me and thus helped me on my journey to writing this book. By talking to people at networking events, I have been able to expand my horizons and take my research further. I am grateful to everyone that has recommended further reading to me, which I have used in my research and included in the 'further reading' section of this book.

I am particularly thankful to those people who have shared their very personal stories with me so that I could include them in this book. A huge 'thank you' therefore goes out to Derek Charnley, Kath Doyle, Ashley Fairburn, Jackie D Frith, Marc Hodgson, Lisa Johnson, Cheryl Kerner, Tracie Lawson, Julie Poland, Fran Sykes and Ashley Wilson.

There are no words powerful enough to thank all the medical and support staff who have helped and supported us and our daughters over the years: all the staff at Birmingham Children's Hospital (Outpatients,

Intensive Care, Cardiology), Doncaster Royal Infirmary (Maternity Ward, Delivery Suite, Special Care Baby Unit and Accident and Emergency), Women's Hospital at Queen Elizabeth Hospital, Edgbaston, Birmingham (Maternity Ward, Delivery Suite, Special Care Baby Unit), Dunsville Medical Centre and Leeds General Infirmary (Paediatric Intensive Care Unit, Paediatric Cardiology). I will also be eternally grateful to my midwife, Angela Taylor, for saving Hannah's life in 1999.

Life does get tough at times and I owe a lot of gratitude to all my friends who have helped in practical and emotive terms over the years. In particular, there are friends who have known me for a very long time and have stuck with me through thick and thin. Claire Russon and Nadège Leonhard, who have been in my life since very early childhood, Clare Storrow who has been my rock and the person giving me a proverbial 'kick up the backside' when I've needed one from time to time, and Claire Eckert who I was lucky enough to meet in a past job and has remained in my life as a trusted and much-loved friend ever since. Julie Poland is one of the newest friends in my life; she met me at one of my low points and was there for me when I needed a shoulder to cry on. I am grateful that she could see the happy person beneath the tears and had the patience to wait for me to re-emerge.

Most of all, I am grateful to my family. My mother and Simon's mother for all the help and support – financial and practical – that they have given us whenever we have needed it and in whatever measure they were able to give it. Much gratitude also to both our sisters for being there for us when we needed practical support and to both our extended families for any help they have given us whenever we have needed it. I am immensely grateful for everyone in my life that has listened to me rambling on about happiness and about the writing of this book and put up with me being absorbed in my task, at times to the exclusion of much else. For this and for so, so much more, I am eternally grateful to my wonderful husband, Simon. For cooking when I was too busy, for not complaining when I 'shushed' him because I was busy writing, for reading sections of the book and offering suggestions for improvement, and generally for being the wonderful man that he is and making it possible for me to do what I do.

More than anything, I am grateful to my fantastic daughters, Charlie and Hannah, for being who they are. For being in my life and making it so rich and funny and, yes, challenging. For taking everything in their strides, for being so mature and dealing with the blows that life has dealt them in the way that they do. For being such a huge inspiration to anyone that meets them and most of all to me. For putting up with me needing so much peace and quiet to write when they wanted to chat, giggle and play with their friends in the house. For allowing me to write about them in the first place, and for lighting up my life. Thank you.

Further Reading (Suggestions) – in alphabetical order

Shaun Achor, 'The Happiness Advantage: The Seven Principles that Fuel Success and Performance at Work', Virgin Digital, 2011

Brené Brown, 'Daring Greatly: how the Courage to Be Vulnerable Transforms the Way We Live, Love, Parent and Lead', Gotham Books, 2012

Viktor E. Frankl, 'Man's Search for Meaning. An Introduction to Logotherapy. With a new foreword by Harold S. Kushner and a new biographical afterword by William J. Winslade', Beacon Press, 1963-2007 (A revised edition of From Death-Camp to Existentialism)

Elizabeth Gilbert, 'Eat Pray Love. One Woman's Search for Everything', Bloomsbury, 2006

Sonja Lyubomirsky, 'The How of Happiness: A Practical Guide to Getting the Life You Want', Piatkus, 2010

David Molden and Pat Hutchinson, 'Brilliant NLP: What the most successful people know, say and do', Pearson/Prentice Hall Business, 2006

Karl Moore, 'The 18 Rules of Happiness: Simple, everyday attitudes for enjoying profound happiness in your life', Inspire3 Publishing, 2009

Matthieu Ricard, The Art of Happiness: A Guide to Developing Life's Most Important Skill', Atlantic Books, 2003 (Translation by Jesse Browner, 2006)

Nigel Risner, 'The Impact Code: Live the Life You Deserve', Capstone, 2006

Gretchen Rubin, 'The Happiness Project, Or, Why I spent a Year Trying to Sing in the Morning, Clean My Closets, Fight Right, Read Aristotle and Generally Have More Fun', HarperCollins eBooks, 2009

Debra Searle, 'The Journey: How to Achieve Against the Odds', Shoal Projects Ltd, 2007

Martin E. P. Seligman, 'Authentic Happiness: Using the New Positive Psychology to Realise Your Potential for Lasting Fulfilment', Nicholas Brealey Publishing, 2003

About the Author

Of dual Italian and German nationalities, Frederika Roberts was born in Italy but grew up in Luxembourg. She moved to the U.K. in 1990 to study Business and Management at the University of Bradford, where she met her husband. She lives in Yorkshire with her husband and two teenage daughters.

Frederika's career has spanned from teaching to social media marketing via recruitment, from voice-over work and radio presenting to professional speaking.

Her book 'Twitter and Facebook Essentials' was published on Kindle in April 2013.

Also by Frederika Roberts

Twitter and Facebook Essentials (Kindle edition), 2013

About the Publishers
The Solopreneur Ltd is a publishing company that focuses on the needs of each individual author. This book has been published through their 'Solopreneur Self-Publishing' (SSP) brand, which enables the author to have complete control over their finished book, but with access to the superior advice and services usually reserved for the traditionally published print, and that are required to create a quality book. Please note, however, that ultimately final editorial approval and decisions rest solely with the author.

For more information on The Solopreneur (Publishing) Ltd go to: www.thesolopreneur.co.uk and for a full list of publishing services go to: www.getthatbookwritten.co.uk